Up to Jerusalem
Where
He Must Suffer

Up to Jerusalem Where He Must Suffer

Sermons and Dialogs for Lent

**by Richard E. Bauerle
and Frederick W. Kemper**

Publishing House
St. Louis

Concordia Publishing House, St. Louis, Missouri
Copyright © 1979 Concordia Publishing House
Manufactured in the United States of America

Library of Congress Cataloging in Publication Data

Bauerle, Richard, 1928-
    Up to Jerusalem where He must suffer.

    1. Lenton sermons. 2. Bible. O. T. Psalms—
Sermons. 3. Dialogue sermons. 4. Lutheran Church—
Sermons. 5. Sermons, American. I. Kemper, Frederick
W., joint author. II. Title.
BV4277.B343   252'.62   79-17148
ISBN 0-570-03795-6

CONTENTS

Lenten Sermons on the Psalms of Ascent

by Richard E. Bauerle

Foreword

"Behold, we are going up to Jerusalem." How many of Jesus' countrymen uttered that intention with great anticipation and joy as they set out to make the yearly Passover pilgrimage to that capital set on Mt. Zion! Over the centuries since the time of David, a pattern had developed as the families gathered in the villages and towns to be joined by others making their way up to Jerusalem. It was an occasion for celebration as well as solemn remembrance of the deliverance from Egyptian slavery.

Our Lord Himself made the trip a number of times. We know what happened when He was twelve and the joyful family occasion turned suddenly anxious.

And then during His ministry the future Paschal Lamb trekked the dusty roads with His companions up a road that inclined steadily for some 14 miles. Along the way, the pilgrims would pause occasionally to rest and to sing the ancient Psalms of Ascent. Jesus knew these songs well. They were an annual reminder of the last journey He would make to Jerusalem, especially poignant in their application to His life and work and death.

Author Richard E. Bauerle invites his readers and hearers to join him as he hears Christ say, "Behold, we are going up to Jerusalem," and rehearses the Psalms of Ascent the Lamb of God recited with profound meaning on the way to the Altar of the Cross.

The Publisher

1

Leaving the Slanderers to God

There are a group of psalms which are linked together in the Psalter called the Songs of Ascent, or the Pilgrim Psalms. These 15 psalms (Psalms 120-134) have not only been of great inspiration to God's people through the ages, but they have been used for strength and comfort in difficult days. They speak of Jerusalem, that Holy City into which pilgrims came and went throughout the centuries. Time and again those pilgrims, marching to that Holy City, would sing those songs of Zion as they came from all over the world to worship the God who brought them out of bondage into their Promised Land. These psalms were used by the chosen of God on the journey to Jerusalem.

Of great significance to us is the fact that Jesus seems to have used these Psalms of Ascent from time to time also. They were undoubtedly very familiar to Him, as they were to most of the Hebrews. There were even occasions, as He spoke to His disciples on His last journey to Jerusalem, when Jesus seemed to set Himself right in the middle of these psalms and made them His personal possession, as if they were written only for Him on the occasion of His passion. Thus they were used also by this Chosen One of God on His journey to the cross where He would make atonement for the sins of the world.

Most of these psalms were written by David. Can't you just see David writing them and using them on one of the great occasions of his life? He was about to bring the Ark of the Covenant into Jerusalem after he had made Jerusalem his capital city. This was the same ark which was built by Moses when the Children of Israel were on their way from Egypt to the Promised Land. God had promised to speak to Moses from that ark, and whenever Moses wished to speak to God, he would go to the ark and God would speak to him out of it. The people of God always felt that if the ark was with them, God was with them and would give them success.

But as the years passed, that ark was used by Israel in an unholy manner. It became for them a temptation to sin. They came to feel that they could do anything they wished as long as they had that ark in their midst. It had become a tool of superstition. They felt free to sin and worship false gods whenever they pleased as long as they had that ark. God would be with them and bless them, they felt, just as long as they did not lose the ark.

One day the Israelites took the ark with them into battle with the Philistines. But Israel lost the battle anyway, and the ark was captured. Now the Philistines had it! It is a long story how they got it back (Psalm 132 refers to it), but many years later, when David became king and made Jerusalem his capital, he decided to bring it into his capital city.

On that great day of procession, David gathered his army together. He also called for his trumpeters, his harpists, his timbrel players, his cymbal players, the players of stringed instruments, and his choirs. There they stood, by the thousands, surrounding the Ark of the Covenant down there at the bottom of the hills, looking up at the hills where Jerusalem stood, and they began singing and playing psalms. As they marched further up the hills toward Mount Zion, they would stop and sing another psalm, until they stood within the walls of Jerusalem, and there they finished singing and playing. Although we cannot be certain these Psalms of Ascent were used for this occasion, yet from the name they have been given, and the message they present, these would have been ideal for that procession up that holy hill.

These psalms were also used by the Hebrews when they came from their communities to worship in Jerusalem. They did not worship there every week. On ordinary sabbaths they would worship in their local synagogs. Worship in the temple was a matter of once or twice or perhaps three times a year. They would go there on their Feast of Ingathering, which was in summer when they harvested their firstfruits. They would go again at the Feast of Tabernacles, when all the harvest had been gathered (like our Thanksgiving Day). But their greatest day of worship was on the Passover, when they celebrated their day of independence from bondage in Egypt.

They would go together as whole communities to worship in their religious and national capital, and as they would go, they would stop along the way and sing these psalms. That is why one of those psalms reads: "How good and pleasant it is when brothers dwell in unity" (Ps. 133:1). Or another says: "I was glad when they said to me, 'Let us go to the house of the Lord'" (Ps. 122:1). That is why, too, when Jesus told His disciples in Jericho: Let us go up to Jerusalem to celebrate the Passover, there were such crowds around Him. The crowds were so great that when Jesus was on His way from Jericho to Jerusalem, two blind beggars could not even make themselves heard above the clamor as they cried out to Jesus. The crowds were going to Jerusalem for the Passover from all over Israel, and they were singing the Psalms of Ascent on the way to the Holy City.

These psalms were used also on other great occasions in Israel's history. When Ezra and Nehemiah brought the Children of Israel back from their bondage in Babylon, they sang the songs of Zion on their way back. They had never forgotten these psalms, and they kept them in their hearts for that moment when they would again approach that city and could sing their great songs without weeping.

Or that day when King Hezekiah was lying sick, about to die, and he called for Isaiah and pleaded with him to call upon the Lord to let him live, Isaiah told him that the Lord would permit him to live 15 years longer. When Hezekiah was well, he went to the temple and sang psalms. Very possibly the Psalms of Ascent.

But, of course, the most meaningful thing about those psalms for us is that they seem to surround the events of the last journey to Jerusalem of the Christ, the Son of David. These were undoubtedly psalms He used as He journeyed from Jericho to Jerusalem to die for the sins of the world. At Jericho He turned to His disciples and said: "Behold, we are going up to Jerusalem; and the Son of Man will be delivered to the chief priests and the scribes, and they will condemn Him to death, and deliver Him to the Gentiles; and they will mock Him, and spit upon Him, and scourge Him, and kill Him; and after three days He will rise" (Mark 10:33-34).

Imagine our Savior, then, as a pilgrim, standing in Jericho, looking around, getting ready to begin His journey to Jerusalem, where He would redeem the world by suffering at the hands of His enemies. The words of Ps. 120 must have come to His mind. Listen to them (KJV):

In my distress I cried unto the Lord, and He heard me.
Deliver my soul, O lord, from lying lips and from a deceitful tongue. What shall be given unto thee? or what

shall be done unto thee, thou false tongue? Sharp arrows of the mighty, with coals of juniper. Woe is me that I sojourn in Mesech, that I dwell in the tents of Kedar! My soul hath long dwelt with him that hateth peace. I am for peace; but when I speak, they are for war.

This was the first psalm pilgrims spoke while still at home as they prepared to begin their journey to Jerusalem. "Lord," they would say, "I am calling upon You to deliver me from these people around me who have lied about me and slandered me. What can I do about them? I can do nothing. But Lord, You can, and Your sharpest arrows and Your hottest anger is reserved for those liars with whom I must live."

Can't you just hear an Israelite saying that, one living in bondage there in Babylon, getting ready to make his journey back to Jerusalem? And can't you just hear Jesus beginning His journey to the cross with that psalm?

That lying tongue! What can you do with it? As the psalmist talks about it, he is at a loss to know what to do about the liar. Indeed, what can you do with him? "What shall be done unto thee, thou false tongue?" he says. There is just nothing we can do about it! Who can slander a slanderer? An honest person just cannot touch him! He fights with weapons an honest person cannot touch. The liar is like a cuttlefish who surrounds himself with an inky blackness into which an honest person cannot penetrate. Like the skunk, you cannot get close enough to endure it. The only level he knows is the lowest of all depths, and an honest person will not go down there to fight. For that reason, the slanderer more often than not escapes unpunished. He goes unpunished by those he has injured the most. His crime, in a very real sense, becomes his shield. People just do not care to get down there to fight where the liar fights. So what can an honest person do?

What can be done with that lying tongue? Ah, the psalmist knows, and he says it here. The sharpest arrows of the Almighty are reserved for slanderers. The coals of juniper shall be piled on them! So here is what he will do. He will depart from them for a while and go to the temple of God. He will leave these people to God, and God will take care of them. What an honest person cannot do, God will do! The sharp arrows of the Almighty will strike them. The worst and quickest punishment is reserved for them. Those coals of juniper were the quickest-burning, the hottest-burning, and the longest-burning of all fuel, and these will be piled on those liars and slanderers.

Only God can bring such punishment. When John looked into heaven as he describes it in the Book of Revelation, three times he says that there are no liars in heaven. The hell of fire is reserved for them! So what shall I do with those liars and slanderers? I will be silent! I will leave them to God. I will go from them to the temple of God, and while I am gone to the temple, God will shoot those liars and slanderers with His sharpest arrows and burn them with His hottest fire. It is much better for me to be the victim of slander than the author of it!

Look! There He stands! Jesus is on trial before His accusers! They have nothing against Him for which to try Him for death, but they have determined that He must die. So they bring in more false witnesses to testify that He said He would tear down the temple and in three days would rebuild it again. All this they said and more. But Jesus did not speak! He remained silent! "Like a sheep that before its shearers is dumb, so He opened not His mouth" (Is. 53:7).

How could He remain silent? Why doesn't He say something? Why doesn't He defend Himself? Why? Well, first of all, because He had the most important job that any man ever had— to reconcile the world to God with His precious blood. So He could be silent in anticipation of that awful weight. But He was also silent because an honest man cannot go down into those depths and fight on that level. It is too awful down there. It is too slimy. It is too slippery. What can Jesus do? He will leave them. He will leave the liars and slanderers to the Lord and be silent. He will go in silence to the cross to bear the weight of the sins of the world.

Now the next psalm breaks in. What will the psalmist do?

I will lift up mine eyes unto the hills, from whence cometh my help. My help cometh from the Lord, who made heaven and earth. He will not suffer thy foot to be moved; He that keepeth thee will not slumber. Behold, He that keepeth Israel shall neither slumber nor sleep. The Lord is thy keeper; the Lord is thy shade upon thy right hand. The sun shall not smite thee by day, nor the moon by night. The Lord shall preserve thee from all evil; He shall preserve thy soul. The Lord shall preserve thy going out and thy coming in from this time forth, and even for evermore (Ps. 121 KJV).

So, looking up, he settles down in peace, and he gets hold of himself. The people of the world will have their day, but I will look to those heights, and I will walk toward those heights, and my foot will not slip, because He who neither slumbers nor sleeps will be at my right hand, and He will preserve my going out and my coming in from this day forward and for evermore.

And isn't it the truth? When I go out in youth to begin life, and come in at the end to die, I shall be preserved. When I go to my grave to sleep, I will come out to awaken, for He who neither slumbers nor sleeps will preserve my life from this day forward and for evermore. What will I do when the slanderer and the liar persecutes me and utters all sorts of falsehood against me? I will be silent and look unto the hills, from whence cometh my help. . . . Especially will I look to that hill of Golgotha, where my silent Savior died for my sins.

2

Beginning the Journey
with Prayer and Trust

It is now time to leave their community. The slanderer is now out of their minds. They have turned him over to the Lord, and they begin their trek toward the hills in their anticipation of seeing that city of Jerusalem which is set in a kind of saucer inside the top of those hills. They have just sung the first two Psalms of Ascent before beginning their journey, looking toward the hills, and then as they begin moving, they look at the crowd around them and they say: "I was glad when they said unto me, let us go into the house of the Lord. Our feet shall stand within thy gates, O Jerusalem" (Ps. 122:1-2 KJV).

What a pleasant thought for God's people! What a pleasant thought for the chosen of the Lord, to be able to go together to the house of the Lord to pray, to communicate with this great God whose name is Love, to be able to worship together and sing the great songs of Zion, to hear of the great love of God, who has given peace to His chosen ones. The word "Jerusalem" means "The City of Peace," and that's what they were going to find there.

As they then begin to climb that steep ascent, these psalms remind them to say to themselves: "There are two things which we must do before we enter into God's presence. We must pray, and we must trust." That is what the next two Psalms of Ascent, Psalms 122 and 123, try to remind them to do: pray and trust. They turn to one another and say: "Pray for the peace of Jerusalem" (Ps. 122:6)—pray for the peace of the City of Peace. And as they walk further up that mountain, they say: "Peace be within thy walls, and prosperity within thy palaces" (Ps. 122:7 KJV).

Can't you just see those Israelites during those long and turbulent years of their history, praying for the peace of Jerusalem? When the Assyrians attacked it and built trenches around it, they prayed for the peace of Jerusalem, and in one night 185,000 of those Assyrians died out there beyond the walls in a plague, and the rest fled. Or when Babylon came down from the north, and laid up a siege for three years so that nothing, and no one, could come in or go out, and the people died of hunger by the thousands until, as Jeremiah said, parents ate their own children for food . . . can't you just hear them praying for the peace of Jerusalem? Or coming back from those years of bondage in Babylon, can't you hear them singing: "Our feet shall stand within thy gates, O Jerusalem" (KJV)?

This psalm has never stopped being used by God's people. but it was especially a psalm for Jesus. It is utterly fascinating how Luke seems to take this psalm and put Jesus inside of it and let that psalm revolve around Him, for listen how it begins: "I was glad when they said to me, let us go to the house of the Lord" (Ps. 122:1).

Luke says that Jesus turned to His disciples and said: "Behold, we are going up to Jerusalem, and everything that is written of the Son of man by the prophets will be accomplished. For He will be delivered to the Gentiles, and will be mocked and shamefully treated and spit upon; they will scourge Him and kill Him, and on the third day He will rise" (Luke 18:31-33). It is the terminology of the psalm to put it this way: "There thrones for judgment were set, the thrones of the house of David" (Ps. 122:5). And there it was that they sat in judgment upon Jesus. It was there that Caiaphas said, "It is expedient . . . that one man should die for the people" (John 11:50). The thrones of judgment were there.

Then the psalm breaks in: "Pray for the peace of Jerusalem" (Ps. 122:6). And here comes Jesus into that city where judgment was to be made upon Him, over the top of Mount Olivet, looking down into that saucer which was Jerusalem, and as He prays this psalm, His voice chokes on the words, "The peace of Jerusalem" . . . and He breaks off, tears streaming down His face, saying: "Would that even today you knew the things that belong to your peace! But now they are hid from your eyes" (Luke 19:42).

Then He goes back to the psalm: "Pray for the peace of Jerusalem." Ah, yes, "For my brethren and companions' sake I will say, Peace be within you . . . and security within your towers" (Ps. 122:7). And then He chokes off again saying: Ah, "The days shall come upon you, when your enemies will cast up a bank upon you and surround you, and hem you in on every side, and dash you to the ground, you and your children within you, and they will not leave one stone upon another in you; because you did not know the time of your visitation" (Luke 19:43-44).

Again, back to the psalm quickly! "Pray for the peace of Jerusalem . . . for the sake of the house of the Lord our God." Anger began building in Him! "I will pray, and I will weep, but I will act too, for the sake of the house of the Lord which is there!" Straight to the house of the Lord He went, whip in His hand, driving out the money changers and the people who sold there! The zeal for the house of the Lord sent Him into a rage over what had happened to that house, and with choked-up throat and tears in His eyes He had to say to them as He whipped them out and overturned their tables: "My house shall be a house of prayer, but you have made it a den of robbers" (Luke 19:46). "How can there be peace within these walls when there are robbers within the temple?"

So He cleansed the temple that day, and cleansed it again from the cross so that people could again with joy sing this psalm: "I was glad when they said to me, 'Let us go to the house of the Lord'" . . . a house cleansed by His own blood.

Having thus prayed for the peace of Jerusalem, the pilgrims continue their ascent. This time they look beyond the hills ahead of them and say: "To thee I lift up my eyes, O thou who art enthroned in the heavens! Behold, as the eyes of servants look to the hand of their master, as the eyes of a maid to the hand of her mistress, so our eyes look to the Lord our God, till He have mercy upon us" (Ps. 123:1-2). On their journey, first they pray for peace, and then they turn in trust to God, knowing that mercy will come from His hand.

They are coming closer to the temple now. They sense the presence of the Lord as they approach the place of worship. Although they knew that the Lord was always near them, yet the temple had a special sense of His presence, and a trust in Him began to well up in them. Chills began coursing up and down their spines. As they get nearer to the temple, their trust in Him increases.

Do you remember how Jesus used to trust God? He was always so close to His Father. He used to say things like: "Do you not know I must be in My Father's house?" (Luke 2:49). "I and the Father are one" (John 10:30). "The Father knows Me and I know the Father" (John 10:15). Once He prayed before the grave of Lazarus: "Father, I thank Thee that Thou hast heard Me" (John 11:41). He always trusted His Father so much!

But there came a day . . . a moment . . . when He lost His

confidence in His Father. It was that moment on the cross when He said: "My God, My God, why hast Thou forsaken Me?" (Matt. 27:46). He didn't even call Him "Father" then. It was now "My God." He had become Sin, and at that moment His Father had forsaken Him, for the Lord hates sin, so He hated His own Son at that moment.

Although that will never happen to us, for that act of redemption was done once and for all on the cross for us, yet there are times when it seems that the Lord is very far away. A pastor friend of mine lay dying, and said, "God seems so far away." Then it is that trust becomes even more precious. God may not prove His love for me every day, but He proved it to me once and for all when He sent His Son into the world. That one act of God is of such dimension that it dwarfs all else. He is close to us even when we cannot feel Him. That one act of God when He became a man and was obedient even unto death, is of such magnitude that I am able to trust Him for all things. That is why I can say with the psalmist: "My heart is steadfast, O God. My heart is steadfast" (Ps. 57:7). And I am always able to say with Job: "Though He slay me, yet will I trust in Him" (Job 13:15 KJV).

This psalm says it so well: "Behold, as the eyes of servants look to the hand of their master, as the eyes of a maid to the hand of her mistress, so our eyes look to the Lord our God, till He have mercy upon us" (Ps. 123:2). The orientals did not speak to their servants very often. Those servants and masters alike were trained to use their hands to signal with, and the good servant always knew what every gesture meant. If the master waved his hand in a certain way, it meant one kind of service to be rendered. If he moved it another way, it meant another kind of service. If he motioned softly, beckoning the servant to come forward, the servant knew the master was about to reward him. So the good servant never took his eyes off his master, lest he miss the gesture of his hand, for the master would never call out, he would only beckon with his hand. So the servant watched and waited, and watched some more, never peering to the right or left so that he could see every movement of the master. That is why the psalmist said: As the eyes of servants look to the hand of their master, so we look to the Lord our God until He has beckoned us to mercy.

Thus it was that my Lord, the Christ, set His eyes steadfastly toward Jerusalem. His heart was steadfast! He had made His decision what He must do, for His Father was His master. His Father was beckoning Him to Jerusalem to die for the sins of the world, and His eyes never left the hand of His master who was beckoning Him on. His eyes were on Jerusalem, where the Lord was about to make the great sacrifice for the sins of the world. As Isaac followed his father Abraham up Mount Moriah where Abraham was willing to sacrifice him, not knowing what was happening, Isaac said, "Father, where is the sacrifice?" His father answered, "The Lord will provide one." It was not so with Jesus! He knew! He had been in the bosom of the Father from the foundation of the world, and He knew! He knew what that sacrifice was to be, so He just fixed His eyes on His Father and went up that hill to which His Father was beckoning Him.

While the Israelites may well look to the Father for mercy, it was now that Jesus was to become the instrument of that mercy. This day He was being beckoned to serve and to die so that the Lord would be able to have mercy on others.

Jesus was following the beckoning hand of His Father. There was no turning back. His heart was steadfast! He would watch the hands of His Father as Jerusalem called. Oh, He would plead again for mercy for Himself, and He would say: "My Father, if it be possible, let this cup pass from Me" (Matt. 26:39). But mercy was not for Him! Not this day! "Nevertheless," He said, "not as I will but as Thou wilt" (Matt. 26:39). Though You slay Me, yet will I trust You! My heart is fixed on You! Whatever You want, I will do, for I know You will yet show mercy.

The next day He carried that cross up that hill, and even though He could not carry it all the way, and He stumbled under that load, He still carried it as far as He could, looking beyond the hills. Later that day He said: "Father, into Thy hands I commend My spirit." He could now in trust see the hand of His Father beckoning Him home. The suffering, trusting Servant saw the Father's hand gently beckoning Him to receive His reward.

Now, because of His trust, that suffering Servant has become my Master. From that cross, as I watch His hands nailed there, outstretched over a darkened sky, He beckons me to follow after Him. Even the tips of His fingers beckon me to be His own and live under Him in His kingdom.

One of the most moving books I have ever read was one entitled *Joni*. It is the true story of a girl, Joni, who writes about her experience. Just after she had graduated from high school, she went swimming in Chesapeake Bay, dove into the water where it was too shallow, and broke her neck. She was paralyzed for the rest of her life from her neck down. She tells her own story of her great struggle to learn to live with this handicap and to accept it as God's will for her life. She writes of how she lost her faith in Christ for a while because she felt He had permitted this to happen to her. She even wanted to commit suicide, but how could she? She was paralyzed! She asked her friends to do it for her, but they would not. Then she discovered that all she had left was her faith.

She writes how, even after two years, there on her bed in the hospital, she would lie during the long nights wanting to cry, but not daring to because she could not wipe her tears or blow her nose, so she just lay there. She tried to help herself those long nights by trying to imagine Jesus standing there beside her bed comforting her, and she wondered if Jesus understood. How could He know what it was like to be paralyzed . . . lying there not being able to move at all, even to scratch her nose, tied with invisible cords to her bed?

Then one night it occurred to her! When Jesus died for her, He hung there on a cross, also not being able to move a muscle! He too could not wipe away His tears, for His arms were fastened to the end of a cross. He too could not move His body to ease His pain, or shift His weight to relieve the ache. He too was paralyzed! He too was immobile! He too was helpless! He too could not scratch His nose! Then the passage from the Letter to the Hebrews came to her which said: "We do not have a high priest who is unable to sympathize with our weaknesses, but we have one who has been tempted in every way, just as we are . . ." (Heb. 4:15 NIV). That thought gave her comfort.

One of the many reasons why I am so grateful that He has called me to be His own is because of the way He beckons me to come to Him, from many places—even from a cross, where mercy has been shown me.

3

Pausing to Remember

As the pilgrims continued their journey up that ascent to Jerusalem, they would stop from time to time and sing another psalm, not just because they wanted to sing praises but because they were trying to catch their breath from the climb. There they would linger a while, and as thcy did, they would remember. Memories would come flooding into their minds, for they would remember other pilgrims who had climbed that same ascent as they approached the Holy City.

It was easy for them to remember because they had had a great and turbulent history. It was made even easier for them to remember because of the psalm they used with which to remember. As they rested a while, they stopped to sing Psalm 124, and memories would come flooding into their minds because the psalm urged them to remember: Children of Israel, remember; do not go into Jerusalem to worship God until you remember! So they sang: "If it had not been the Lord who was on our side, now may Israel say; if it had not been the Lord who was on our side, when men rose up against us, then they had swallowed us up quick, when their wrath was kindled against us" (Ps. 124:1-3 KJV).

Ah, memories! How could we worship God without them? When we remember, our hearts become clean again as we see how God has blessed us, and we try a little harder to be what we ought to be. Memory is that angel with the backward look which makes all the treasures of the past ours again. It is what lets us have roses in December. It is extremely important that we keep our memories clear so that we do not forget what the Lord has done. We thus remember: If the Lord had not been on our side . . . say it again . . . if the Lord had not been on our side when men rose up against us, they would have swallowed us up quick when their wrath was kindled against us.

The Lord was always on our side, they would say: Even when we rebelled and He punished us for it, He punished us because He was on our side. Even when our ancestors sold their brother Joseph into slavery, the Lord was on their side. Joseph himself said so. When He brought us out of Egypt, it was the Lord who stood between us and Pharoah's army. It was the Lord who opened up the Red Sea for us to cross over on dry land. It was the Lord who punished the evildoers among us because He was for us. And when our enemies rose up against us, the Lord was for us and we won. Ah, if it had not been the Lord who was on our side—let's say it again—if the Lord had not been on our side, our enemies would have swallowed us up quick!

It is striking how the psalmist says: "They would have swallowed us up quick"(KJV). Not quickly, but quick, as when we say "to judge the quick and the dead." Not like a lion devours a prey that is killed by slowly consuming it, but quick, like a shark tears and chews and swallows its prey alive. Yes, we remember how the Lord protected us from that! It wasn't even that we deserved to win. We deserved to lose, but the Lord was on our side, so we won. "Blessed be the Lord, who has not given us as a prey to their teeth" (Ps. 124:6), they said. "We have escaped as a bird from the snare of the fowlers; the snare is broken, and we have escaped!" (Ps. 124:7). My goodness, how can we go into Jerusalem to worship God without remembering what the Lord has done for us because He was on our side? How important that is to remember! Well might we sit here on the side of this mountain overlooking Jerusalem and remind ourselves of that, for the day is coming when we will probably be attacked again, and perhaps lose the battle. But how can we really lose if God is on our side? God is on our side, so winning or losing, we win.

When Jesus was on His last journey with His disciples up that ascent to Jerusalem, singing this psalm with them, He must have begun getting very quiet about now. Knowing that this psalm was written for Him, a vision was beginning to appear before Him stronger and stronger. He could see Himself being surrounded by those ferocious enemies who wanted to swallow Him up quick, for even now the soldiers began to gather and the rulers were even now assembling themselves against Him. The false witnesses were already now being prepared, and already He was beginning to feel those spikes being driven into His hands and feet as His enemies there jeered at Him and buffeted Him.

How important it must have been for Him, sitting there resting on that journey, to repeat this psalm: If the Lord had not been on our side . . . if the Lord had not been on our side . . . and then using the last verse of this psalm: "Our help is in the name of the Lord, who made heaven and earth" (Ps. 124:8).

There He sits, resting with His disciples, very quiet now as He is thinking about generations yet unborn who would be able to say because of Him: Had not the Lord been on our side, He would never have died for me—let's say it again—had not the Lord been on our side, He would never have died for me. Our help is in the name of the Lord, because He died for me. Our soul has escaped as a bird out of a snare, for the snare is broken and we have escaped, because He died for me! Everything is working together for my good because the Lord is on my side, for He died for me.

As I meditate on this, I realize that, as at no other time, Jesus became my Lord when He died for me, for He was on my side! When His enemies rose up against Him, He took it because He was on my side! When those wild beasts began tearing His body apart, He was on my side, so He took it! When the rabble said to Him up there on the cross, "If you are the Son of God, come down from the cross," He did not come down, because He was on my side and He died for me there! He became my Lord there! Now I don't have anything, anywhere to fear, for I know the Lord is on my side. Even when He says things that may frighten me, I can take them and rejoice in them, for He is on my side. Even when He says such frightening things as He said that very day to His disciples from Mt. Olivet, I am able to rejoice in them, for He is on my side.

Matthew 24 records that as Jesus overlooked that city, His disciples asked Him when all of those things were going to happen that He had talked about, and He said to them (quietly and slowly): "You will hear of wars and rumors of wars; see that you are not alarmed; for this must take place. . . . For nation will rise against nation, and kingdom against kingdom, and there will be famines and earthquakes in various places: all this is but the beginning of the birth-pangs. Then they will deliver you up to tribulation, and put you to death; and you will be hated . . . for My name's sake. And then many will fall away, and betray one another, and hate one another. . . . And . . . most men's love will grow cold." He then went on to describe all the desolations that will take place with great tribulation, and (in Luke 21) He concluded: "When these things begin to take place, look up and raise your heads, because your redemption is drawing near." How strange that He would say, in effect, that when these things begin taking place, remember, it is for you! God is doing it for you! God is on your side.

I find that terribly hard to accept, that when all of these things happen, it is for my sake. But when I see my God hanging on that cross, then I can believe this—that God is on my side, whatever happens. When I see the desolations and famines and wars—oh, how I hate the thought of that—yet, He who died for me said that it is for me, so I believe it. No wonder Paul could say with such ecstasy: "What then shall we say to this? If God is for us, who is against us? He who did not spare His own Son but gave Him up for us all, will He not also give us all things with Him? . . . Who shall separate us from the love of God? Shall tribulation, or distress, or persecution, or famine, or nakedness, or peril, or sword? . . . No, in all these things we are more than conquerors through Him who loved us" (Rom. 8:31-37). There it is again! It is for us because God is for us. Ah yes, we just have to remember: If God were not on our side, say it again, if God were not on our side when men rose up against us, they would have swallowed us up quick.

But God is on our side. That is why those pilgrims on the ascent to Jerusalem, having rested for a while, and having thought about what God had done for them, now arise to begin their journey again. They are approaching Jerusalem now, knowing that God had blessed them and would bless them again. As they looked at that walled, fortified city, they said in the words of the next psalm: "They that trust in the Lord shall be as Mount Zion, which cannot be removed but abideth forever. As the mountains are round about Jerusalem, so the Lord is round about His people from henceforth, even forever" (Ps. 125:1-2 KJV).

That must be quite a scene, coming down over Mt. Olivet, looking toward the city of Jerusalem. High hills all around the city, and then a valley (the valley of Kidron), and then another hill, in which the city of Jerusalem sits. When that wall was around Jerusalem, there was no way anyone could get in unless they were invited. Even when Nebuchadnezzar attacked that city with overwhelming military strength, he could not get in. The city was too well protected by walls and mountains. That city finally fell, but not because Nebuchadnezzar beat it down—only because he laid a siege around it for three full years.

You just could not get in unless you were invited. "Those who trust in the Lord are like Mount Zion, which cannot be moved." Why, those fortifications of that city were such that even when the Lord wanted it to fall, it took three years for it to fall! It was so entrenched, so established that it could not be taken.

What a picture of God's chosen! They cannot be taken! They cannot be moved! They are like Mount Zion! How blessedly simple: Others may work at iniquity, he says, but peace shall be upon God's people (Ps. 125:5). Entrenched! Established by God! And so at peace. God's people, secure in the knowledge that God is for them and has protected them in such a way that nothing can harm them.

There is a familiar story in the Old Testament about how Syria once attacked Samaria while Elisha was the prophet there. The servant of Elisha was beside himself. What are we to do? he said to Elisha; the enemy is all around us, and we will all be dead by morning. Elisha just sat there in total peace and prayed to God: "Lord, open his eyes that he may see." And God did open the eyes of the servant, and the servant looked at the hills around Samaria, and there he saw what Elisha had seen. All over the mountains he saw the angels and chariots of God protecting the city. No wonder Elisha could say to him in confidence and peace: See, He who is for us is stronger than he who is against us. It was true, for the Syrians were struck blind.

Although St. Paul compares the Christian life to an athletic contest, that comparison must not be pushed too far. In an athletic contest you must strain and struggle to win, and then half the time you lose anyway. In some ways the Christian life is more like sitting in a fortified city that cannot be moved. If an enemy strikes, he is struck blind, and we just watch him as he stumbles and falls. We just wait in peace. They that wait upon the Lord shall be like Mt. Zion; they shall never be moved.

That is why Jesus could stand before His tormentors, and while they nervously lied, and struck Him in the face, and nearly went into a frenzy, and plaited for Him a crown of thorns, and whipped Him, He just stood there! Even Pilate was so frustrated at His peace of mind that he finally said: "You will not speak to me? Do You not know that I have power to release You, and power to crucify You?" And Jesus quietly said: "You would have no power over Me unless it had been given you from above" (John 19:10-11).

That was all He said. Why should He say more? He had just that week looked at that city from the hill and said: "They who trust in the Lord are like Mount Zion, which cannot be moved." Why? Well, because the Lord is on our side.

4

Justifying Our Dreams

As the pilgrims again begin their ascent with their friends and their families, it is fortunate for them that the next two psalms of David, (Pss. 126 and 127) speak as they do. It gives the pilgrims the opportunity to draw their families together and speak to one another about what God has done for them and about what they mean to each other. These two psalms present to the pilgrims the opportunity to be a little sentimental. They speak to each other lovingly about their dreams, about laughter and singing, and about how glad they are to have each other. It is nice to have moments like that with your family. It is like going through a scrapbook that has been forgotten for a long time, and opening it together and being surprised all over again at the things you used to do together.

Perhaps it meant more than that to David when he wrote these psalms, as he said: "When the Lord turned again the captivity of Zion, we were like them that dream. Then was our mouth filled with laughter, and our tongue with singing. . . . The Lord has done great things for us, whereof we are glad" (Ps. 126:1-3 KJV).

When he wrote this psalm, David could have been thinking of many different instances when the Lord turned their captivity into laughter. He could have been thinking about that time when the Israelites walked around Jericho seven times the same day, and after their seventh trip around, the trumpeters were ordered to blow their trumpets and the people were to shout, and the wall of Jericho fell. Think of how their shouts turned to laughter! They could not speak. They were stunned. Words were only a mixture of laughter and unbelief. Their speech was garbled with laughter as they struggled to give expression to one another about what was happening.

Or David may have thought of his own experience that day on the plains of Israel when the Philistines brought forth their champion Goliath, a giant nine feet tall, who stood there and laughed at the Israelites and cursed their God and challenged anyone to come out to fight him. When David brought the noon meal to his brothers, he was amazed how the Israelite army was frozen with fear by the taunts of the giant. He said: Who is this infidel that is mocking our God? . . . I will go out and fight him. When Goliath was dead and David had cut off his head, a great roar went up from the camp of the Israelites—a roar of disbelief, laughter, and triumph as they could only shout in unutterable phrases about what had happened. O yes, "When the Lord restored the fortunes of Zion, we were like those who dream. Then our mouth was filled with laughter."

Greek historians tell how, when the Romans had conquered Greece, the Roman consul went to Greece to tell them that all the Greeks were to be free. When this news was given to the citizens of Athens, they could not believe it. They were unable to receive it all at once, so the news had to be given to them a little bit at a time because it was too much to believe. It was too good for them to comprehend all at once.

That was the way the disciples had to be told about the resurrection of Jesus. The news had to be given to the disciples and to the women at the tomb a little bit at a time. They could not absorb it all at once. It was too much for them. Even by evening of that resurrection day, they were still like those in a dream. The women had told them that He had arisen, Mary had spoken to Him, He had appeared to some of His disciples, but even then, when He met two of His disciples on the road to Emmaus and walked with them, they were still in a turmoil because they could not believe what had been told them. They were like men in a dream, and all they could do was laugh when they finally accepted the news. The Lord had turned the captivity of Zion, and they were like those who dream.

I love that picture! It describes how I feel about the death and resurrection of this Lord of mine. I can't quite comprehend what it means for me, but I don't really want to hear any more because I want to hang onto it without someone trying to explain it to me. I am afraid that if someone tried to explain it to me, it would make it harder for me to believe, and instead of convincing me of its truth it might cause me to lose some faith in it. I want to believe it so bad that I don't even want to have anyone try to explain it to me.

I feel a little like Jacob did after all those years when he thought Joseph, his best-loved son, was dead. He was totally convinced that Joseph was dead because his other sons had told him so. Then one day, here came his sons back from Egypt, those same sons who told about Joseph dying, and now told him that Joseph was alive. How could he believe them? He could not! When they brought the things into the house that Joseph had given them, he still could not believe them. Finally, they brought Jacob outside and showed him the chariots of Egypt that Joseph had sent to bring his father there. That is when he said, in effect, "Don't show me any more; I am convinced he is alive." He just did not want to hear any more or see any more for fear that their witness would convince him otherwise.

That is the way I feel about the resurrection. I believe His death was for me, and I believe He arose from the dead so that I and my loved ones will arise, but now don't try to convince me further of it or you may make me have doubts about it! It is such good news that I am like one in a dream about it. I don't even want anyone to try to convince me that it is true. No arguments will convince me. Only the Lord can convince me of its truth, and that He has done. I just want to live with that dream so that my voice will be filled with laughter and my lips with singing. I just want to live with that dream, that Christ died for me and arose for me.

But even more than that, it is not for myself alone that I am allowed to dream. I am allowed to dream even further because of what the next psalm describes. It speaks of my children and the blessing they are to me. Life would be a remarkable thing all by itself, even if there were no life everlasting, and I think I would perhaps be satisfied with life without the hope of eternal life were it not for the fact that I not only live, but I love too. I just have loves that yearn for something more than this life can offer. I not only want to live eternally; I want to love eternally. I want to love and see my ancestors forever. I want to see my parents again. I want to see my wife and my children and my children's children, and I want to be able to love them forever. My love, the greatest of all virtues, will never be satisfied unless I am able to love eternally. That is why the next psalm (Ps. 127) is so precious. It has been called "The Psalm of Ascent for Solomon."

David now turns to his son Solomon, whom he loves so dearly, and says something like this to him: Son, you know that the one great disappointment of my life has been that the Lord did not permit me to build a temple for Him. My hands have blood on them, for I was a man of war, and I had your mother's first husband killed because of my lust for her, so the Lord has said that I am not to build His temple. But you will! So let me tell you this: "Unless the Lord builds the house, those who build it labor in vain. Unless the Lord watches over the city, the watchman stays awake in vain. . . . Lo, sons are a heritage from the Lord, the fruit of the womb a reward. Like arrows in the hand of a warrior are the sons of one's youth. Happy is the man who has his quiver full of them . . ." (Ps. 127:1-5).

Ah yes, our children. What they mean to us! How much we want to tell them! How much advice we have for them! How much we love them! How much we want to tell them that unless they permit the Lord to build their life, they labor in vain trying to make something of it. And unless they call on the Lord to watch over them, they will always be in danger.

It is to his son that David now says that good children are like arrows in the hand of a warrior. They can go where the warrior can't go. The old warrior is limited in what and where he can go. There are places where it is too dangerous to go, but the arrow can go, so he sends it out.

And when that old warrior stands at the gate to fight an enemy, he will not be ashamed, because his sons stand with him and fight with him. Ah, happy is the man who has his quiver full of those arrows. And son, don't fret so much about things. Let the Lord take care of things for you. "It is in vain that you rise up early and go late to rest, eating the bread of anxious toil; for He gives to His beloved sleep" (Ps. 127:2). Just take it easy, son. Do what you can, and let the Lord do the rest.

It appears that Solomon took David's advice. David had two other sons, both very ambitious, both wanting to ascend to the throne of their father. Both fought for it and killed for it. One even attacked his father to take the throne for himself before his father was dead. But Solomon just waited. The throne was his, and he knew it; all he had to do was wait for it. He did not strain for it, he did not toil for it, he did not fret over it. He just waited, and when his father David died, he ascended the throne and became a greater king than his father before him.

And he did build that temple! Whether or not tradition is correct, we are not certain, but tradition has it that Solomon would not permit his workers to work too hard or too long each day on that temple. He took the advice of his father who said: "It is in vain for you to rise up early and go late to rest." He listened and learned from his father that the greatest work is done while one sleeps, for that is when the Lord works for us. He did what he could, and then he let the Lord do the rest. David would have been proud of him had he seen the temple!

How meaningful for us to give this advice to our children! We do what we can, and we let the Lord do the rest. Why, I can't even save myself! I have to let God do that, so I will let God do it—and He takes care of my salvation, completely! I will do what I can in this world, and I will let God do what He can through me. It is useless to rise up early and go to bed late, eating the bread of anxious toil. Let God do what He will do! That is good advice.

"And son," David said, "I am so glad to have you. Children are the gift of the Lord. There is no other gift like you." Isn't that true? We would do anything for our children. They are the reason we want to accumulate some wealth in the world, so we can leave them something. Why build a house if you have no household to leave it to? Why own property if you can't deed it to a loved one? Napoleon could never have built a dynasty because he had no son to will it to. Perhaps that is why he was so careless about his kingdom. Henry VIII went mad because he had no son. How we love our children! How much they mean to us!

That is all the more reason why the atoning death of my Lord and His resurrection mean so much to me and make me dream of it. I want to be with my loved ones forever and ever, for I love them more than I love myself. Life is just not long enough to love them. Life without love is always long enough, but life with love is never long enough.

Jesus knew this. How well He knew this! That last night together with His disciples, He gathered them very close to Him just before He went out into the garden to pray for them, and He said:

> "Little children, yet a little while I am with you. You will seek Me; and as I said to the Jews, now I say to you, 'Where I am going you cannot come.' A new command-ment I give to you, that you love one another; even as I have loved you, that you also love one another. By this all men will know that you are My disciples, if you have love for one another." Simon Peter said to Him: "Lord, where are You going?" Jesus answered, "Where I am going you cannot follow Me now, but you shall follow afterward" (John 13:33-36).

Man, that's for me! I don't want to hear anymore whether that is true or not! I only want to look at that picture of my Lord calling me "My little child" and saying, "Don't be afraid to love, for you will follow Me, and that love will go on into eternity." And I can just see that train . . . my loved ones gone before me, and I following in their train, and my children and their children's children following in my train, and together again there on Mount Zion, singing those songs of Zion in a familiar land with familiar friends.

5

Forgiveness—God's Act for a Purpose

One of the things which impresses us about the Psalms of Ascent is the fact of their inspiration. They were truly inspired by God. The word "inspire" means to "breathe into." When it says that God breathed into Adam the breath of life, He inspired Adam and gave him life. As we read these psalms, we have to use that same word, for God inspired David to write them. David alone, without inspiration, could never have said what these psalms say. This is especially true as we realize that they are so closely related to the last journey which Jesus took with His disciples on the way to Jerusalem to die for the sins of the world. So we again take up those sacred words, totally conscious of the fact that we cannot do justice to them. We can only recite them and draw a few thin threads of inspiration from them.

On their journey to Jerusalem, God's chosen have now come over the top of the Mount of Olives and have come down that mountain into the valley of Kidron and are looking up to the next mountain, on which Jerusalem is located. There they sing out in the words of Psalm 130: "Out of the depths I cry to Thee, O Lord! Lord, hear my voice! Let Thy ears be attentive to the voice of my supplications! If Thou, O Lord, shouldst mark iniquities, Lord, who could stand? But there is forgiveness with Thee, that Thou mayest be feared" (Ps. 130:1-4).

The singing of this psalm down there in the valley is a natural outgrowth of the psalm before (Ps. 129) as they recited in anger their complaint against their enemies. They said: " 'Sorely have they afflicted me from my youth,' let Israel now say— 'Sorely have they afflicted me from my youth, yet they have not prevailed against me. The plowers plowed upon my back; they made long their furrows' " (Ps. 129:1-3). (We can see how appropriate this psalm was for Jesus as He was lashed and whipped.) They would think to themselves: "From my youth, my enemies have beaten me and struck me. They have whipped me with lashes so deep that they made furrows, deep furrows upon my back as a plow cuts a furrow in a field. So have they cut my back with their whips." And in anger and frustration they say: Lord, You take care of it for me! Cut them off! And like grass that grows on a housetop, let them wither and die before they even have to be mowed the first time (cf. Ps. 129:6-7). Then they go on to say: "Out of the depths have I cried unto Thee, O Lord. Lord, hear my voice" (Ps. 130:1 KJV).

Lord, they would say, You know we ourselves are not innocent. We have sinned too. But Lord, if You should count our sins against us, then Lord, who could stand? We all know we have sinned, Lord, but we also know that there is forgiveness with You so that You may be feared. So we will just wait. . . . My soul waits, and in Your word do I hope. My soul waits for the Lord more than they who watch for the morning. I say, more than they who watch for the morning.

How fitting it is after the fury of Psalm 129 that we should read straight on to the stark but serene realism of Psalm 130. Here is one of the most familiar psalms, perhaps the most Christian psalm of all. This psalm has served Christians more than any other down through the ages. This was the psalm Luther used throughout that awful night in that most decisive moment of his life. The story is familiar how he was called to trial by the emperor and the church for his teachings. He was on trial for heresy, and he knew that if he would be found guilty he could be burned at the stake. In the year 1521 he was called to Worms to make his defense. When he stood up to speak in his defense, he was stopped. The conversation and examination went something like this: He was asked, "Luther, are these your writings or not?" Luther answered, "Yes." The examiner then said, "Do you recant them?" Luther said, "I thought I was brought here to defend my works." The prosecutor said, "You have been brought here only to recant your works. Do you recant them or not?" After some hesitation, Luther said, "May I have until tomorrow morning to give my answer?" The prosecutor said, "Tomorrow morning, then."

That night Luther did not sleep, and he said later that this was the psalm he prayed over and over: "Out of the depths I cry to Thee, O Lord! Lord, hear my voice! . . . If Thou, O Lord, shouldst mark iniquities, Lord, who could stand? But there is forgiveness with Thee, that Thou mayest be feared. I wait for the Lord, my soul waits, and in His word do I hope; my soul waits for the Lord more than watchmen for the morning, more than watchmen for the morning" (Ps. 130:1-6).

Some years later, during the persecutions in England, an

entire jail was filled with Protestants, and they were overcome with fears and anxieties until one of their leaders stood up and said, "Come, let us defy the devil and sing a psalm." This was the psalm they sang.

Still later, when John Bunyan was in prison for his faith, he said that he had such difficulty giving expression to his love for God that words would not come to him until he thought of this psalm, and with this psalm he expressed his love for God.

It is the most Christian psalm of all, for it is quite different from the rest of those psalms that ask forgiveness. There are other psalms that we hold very dear which ask for forgiveness; but those other psalms plead for it. This one is quite different. This is not a prayer for forgiveness. It is simply a statement that forgiveness is there and available. That is all. "Forgiveness is mine!" he says. There is no speculation, there is no hoping that God will forgive. It is not even a confession that he is a sinner. It is just a plain statement of fact. "Here I am, and there is God, and God will act on my behalf by forgiving my sin," he says.

You see, it is a Christian message! It was inspired! David was inspired to say something that fits so well into our New Testament times. This is the way the Christian looks at sin. It has been forgiven! I don't have to plead for it. I don't have to mutilate my body to get it. It has been done! Christ has paid the penalty of my sin, and God will not exact payment twice. All I can do about it is receive it. "I will just wait for the Lord. My soul waits for it. It is mine, and the Lord is going to give it to me."

There is something else about this psalm that makes it all the more fascinating. From the studies of ancient Jewish literature it has been discovered that the phrase, "Out of the depths" carried with it great fear. It was a description of the oceans, and the ancient Jews had a great fear of the deep, for it was believed that out of the depths of the sea came a hideous sea monster called "Tehom Rabbah." There was always something sinister about the sea in Jewish literature, as there was in all ancient writings. That is why on ancient maps, drawn before it was discovered that the earth was round, we find written around the edges of the maps on the seas the statement: "Beyond here is evil and the sea monsters." It was something they always feared.

Those miracles of Jesus, then, when He stilled the storm on the sea and when He walked on water become all the more significant. How significant too, is that statement of John when, in the

Book of Revelation, he looks into heaven and sees the New Jerusalem coming down from heaven. He describes the golden streets and the gates of pearl and the walls of jasper, and then he says: "And the sea was no more" (Rev. 21:1). That sea, it was felt, was the curse from which evil came.

What is so startling, then, about this psalm is the direction in which David turns when he calls to God from out of those depths. He says: "If Thou, O Lord, shouldst mark iniquities, Lord, who could stand?" (Ps. 130:3). What is this evil that makes him cry out from the depths? Why, it is his sin! It is iniquity! That is the evil that can rise up and swallow me up! That is what I fear . . . my iniquity . . . this deformity which is a part of me. The word "iniquity" literally means "deformity." That is what I fear. My deformity! I am afraid it will take over my whole life!

Therefore he cries out: "If Thou, O Lord, shouldst mark iniquities, Lord, who could stand? But there is forgiveness with Thee, that Thou mayest be feared" (Ps. 130:3-4). Ah, Lord, what good would I be if You should count my sins against me? Who would be left to praise You, O Lord, if You should count our trespasses against us? Could I praise You from hell, O Lord? No, Lord, if You should count our sins against us, who would be left to praise You? No one! That is why You have forgiven us, isn't it? Because if You didn't, there would be no one to praise You. That's why You can't let our iniquities rise up and swallow us up, can You? There just would not be anyone left to praise You! So I will wait, Lord, for You to redeem me, for with You there is plenteous redemption, and You will redeem us from all our iniquities!

What a marvelously beautiful Christian expression! The Lord wants me to praise Him, but the only way it can ever happen is if He forgives me. He *has* to forgive me if I am to praise Him. So I can rest comfortably in the thought that I am forgiven, and I will just wait for Him to redeem me—my soul doth wait.

There is something more than just the words of the psalm which makes it possible for us to wait so patiently for that forgiveness and redemption. It is the way the Scriptures describe the last few hours of the life of Jesus. The record states that Jesus had sung some psalms with His disciples. (Incidentally, Jesus must have sung often. We wonder what kind of a voice He had, and what His voice and the voices of the fishermen and tax collectors sounded like when they sang together.) Then He went into the garden to pray. No doubt He used the psalms which were so familiar to Him from His youth, and certainly they must have meant everything to Him this night: "All Thy waves and Thy billows have gone over Me" (Ps. 42:7), He would have said. "My tears have been My food day and night, while men say to Me continually, where is Your God?" (Ps. 42:3). And then on the cross, more psalms must have come flooding into His memory: "I say to God, My rock: 'Why hast Thou forsaken Me? Why go I mourning because of the oppression of the enemy?' As with a deadly wound in My body, My adversaries taunt Me, while they continually say, 'Where is Your God?' " (Ps. 42:9-10).

While hanging there on the cross, He looks around and sees those who taunt Him and mock Him, and the soldiers who had spit on Him and plaited a crown of thorns and put it on His head and then nailed Him to the cross, who are now playing dice to see who would get His cloak. He looked around, and we wonder if He thought: "If Thou, O Lord, shouldst mark iniquities, Lord, who could stand? But there is forgiveness with Thee, that Thou mayest be feared" (Ps. 130:3-4). "Lord, who could praise You if You do not forgive them?" So He drew a deep breath and spoke out loud for the first time from the cross: "Father, forgive them, for they know not what they do" (Luke 23:34). "Lord, if You don't forgive them, who would there be to praise You?" And because God's own Son asked for it, that rabble got it!

It was just 50 days after His resurrection, when these same people came back to Jerusalem to celebrate on their next visit to the Holy City, that they were together on the day of Pentecost. Peter stood up in that crowd and told them that this One whom they had crucified was the Son of God and had risen from the dead. They were horrified and humiliated and said to Peter, "What shall we do?" Peter said, "Repent, and be baptized, every one of you, in the name of Jesus Christ for the forgiveness of your sins" (Acts 2:37-38). That day 3,000 of them believed and were saved. The very ones who had asked that He be crucified now praised God because they were forgiven. They were forgiven! Their iniquity was cleansed because God's own Son prayed for it from the cross so that there would be someone left to praise God. That is as great a comfort as I know.

There are many things about this God of ours that fascinate us, not the least of which are the many decisions He makes. Decisions like what He will permit us to discover about Him and how

He does things. Decisions about the universe. These are fascinating things. But even more intriguing are the decisions He makes about who will be what. When He distributes this thing called "life" around this planet, who will be what? Who will live in luxury and who in poverty? That is largely God's decision as He decides where we will live on this planet. Or who will have the capacity to lead, and who will not have that capacity? Or what family will we be born into, or what gifts will we have, or what color will we be, or when will we be born, or when die? Will I be a man or woman, sickly or healthy? God makes all those decisions. And the different forms of life! What will be a dog, or a chicken, or a turkey that will have its head chopped off because someone wants it for a Thanksgiving dinner? Or a snake, or a plant, or a flower? Those are forms of life too. Who will be what? God makes all those decisions, and we so often wonder why He made us a man instead of a dog, because there is life in both which only God can give. It is as someone said: "Isn't life wonderful? I wonder why it happened to me." Just think of the number of decisions God makes every day!

But the fact is, when God makes a decision, it is made! No one can do anything in the world about it. He decides what life will go into a dog and what life will go into a man. He decides when we are to be born, and where, and to what family, and what color, and what sex, and what gifts we are to have. God decides, and there is nothing we can do about it. We may complain, or rejoice, or accept it, or rebel, but we can't do anything about it! Once God has decided, it is decided once and for all and forever.

Out of that, this great thought emerges. God decided what He would do about sin. He decided irrevocably and decisively to send His Son into this world to die for it. It is a decision that God made, and we can do nothing but receive it. We simply have no choice over it, because God made His decision that this is the way the world would be redeemed.

Just think what that means! Irrevocably you and I who receive the Christ as our Savior have been forgiven! God Himself made that decision! It is done! That must be the greatest news in the world! When we come together to worship, that is why we come. We do not come together so that God will make some new decision about us and our sins. We come together to praise God that the decision has been made and we will belong to Him eternally. We only come together to talk about that great decision which He made before He laid the foundations of the world.

Because of God's great decision to forgive my sin, I am now able to look at my death with hope. God decided to forgive me for a purpose. What good would that decision to forgive me be if it were only for this life? In that case I could do without it. But He decided to forgive me so I could be with Him forever and praise Him forever. I don't know what kind of a bargain that is for God, but God is going to get something out of it too, for God loves me and wants me with Him. I will be with Him forever as a forgiven sinner. That decision to love and forgive me is forever!

As I think of my own loved ones who have died, I think to myself that it was nice to have had them with me for a while, and it is nice to have all those memories of them. But the memories of them do not satisfy me. In fact, those memories make me hurt. Only their person with me would satisfy me again, and if I had the power, I would bring them back to live with me.

Here, then, is this God who made me and sustained me throughout this lifetime, and He loved me and forgave me. It must be the same for Him. He has the power to bring me back to life, and I can't see how this God of love could ever say about me, "Well, I was so happy I made him and he gave Me many memories which I will never forget, and I am sorry to have had to lose him." This God of love and forgiveness will never have to say that!

He forgave me for a purpose! He forgave me so that He would have more than memories to hang on to. He forgave me so He could spend eternity with me, because when someone is loved, memories are not enough. Only the person with you is enough. God decided to forgive me forever, and I have the privilege to live with that and die with that. "If Thou, O Lord, shouldst mark iniquities, Lord, who could stand? But there is forgiveness with Thee, that Thou mayest be feared" (Ps. 130:3-4).

6

Humility Answered by Quietness of Heart

When we approach God, we do it in humility. It is now time for the pilgrims to make their final preparations to enter the holy city to worship their God. What were they now to do? What were they to say? The gates of the city were now before them and they were about to enter, so they were given words to say which expressed their feelings. The words are those of a song of humility. How else could they approach God? "Lord," they said, "my heart is not haughty, nor mine eyes lofty; neither do I exercise myself in great matters, or in things too high for me. Surely I have behaved and quieted myself, as a child that is weaned of his mother; my soul is even as a weaned child" (Ps. 131:1-2 KJV).

They had just finished saying, "Out of the depths have I cried unto Thee" (Ps. 130:1 KJV) and then had made that great statement of their faith with the assurance that their sins are forgiven, and now they say in their hearts something like this, as David did when he wrote it: "Lord, since I have been forgiven and counted as so precious in Your eyes, I just lay back in Your everlasting arms and rest there. But You know, Lord, that I do not feel that I am worthy of all that. I am a king before You, I know that; but I am a king because You have made me a king, for I did not earn it. But I am not haughty about it. You know that. You know me, and You know that I accept this kingship humbly. I am not trying to be more than I am. You know this, Lord, for You know my heart. Do You know what I feel like, Lord? I feel like a weaned child who rests quietly at its mother's breast. My soul is quieted within me."

There are some criticisms of this psalm. Some say it should not have been included in the Psalter. They say it is trite and sounds like a man who is proud of his humility. But we must understand that these are the words of a man who is talking to his God. He does not care what people may think of him. This is a matter between him and God, and he knows that God knows his heart. He is not at all concerned about what anyone thinks of him at this point in his communion with God. He is simply saying, "Lord, You know what is in my heart, and I don't care what people may think of me. I am talking to the Lord. It is just You and me, Lord."

David had written this little psalm, and how appropriate it was for him when the ark was taken into Jerusalem, for there he did an astounding thing. In front of this entire company . . . in front of this mass of people who were going up to Jerusalem with him, he took off his clothes, all his royal attire, and asked one of the priests to let him wear one of his cloaks, and there, in front of that mass of people, he danced with all his might, and shouted and sang with the sounds of the trumpets that were being blown. It is obvious that he did not care at this point what anyone thought of him. When he—the anointed representative of God's chosen nation—was praising God, what did it matter what some people thought?

His wife Michal, who had been watching the proceedings out of the palace window as David danced his way to the city gates, was so embarrassed over it that the record states she despised him for what he had done. Later that day, when David came home, he was elated over the proceedings of the day. But that elation was not to last. Michal confronted him and said to him (paraphrased): "Well, you certainly made a fool of yourself today, undressing before your army and the maidens of your servants, and dancing like any vulgar person shamelessly uncovering himself." David said to her: "Just who do you think you are talking to? I am the king whom God has chosen to be king! I did not undress and dance for the people! I did it for the Lord who made me king! I did this to His praise! And I will make merry before the Lord whenever I wish, for it is between me and the Lord that these things were done today. And because you feel contempt towards me because of what I did this day between my Lord and myself, let it be known to you that you will never again by my wife so that you will never have to be ashamed of what I will do again." And it was so. They never lived together again.

Knowing David as we do, how sensitive he was, and how easily hurt he could be, we wonder if he did not go from that confrontation to his balcony in his palace and look out over the landscape and think to himself as he once said: "O that I had wings like a dove! I would fly away from here and be at rest." (Ps. 55:6). "Why is it, Lord, that a day which begins so well, with such joy and elation . . . why is it that such a day so often has to end so badly?"

We wonder also if his mind did not go back to this psalm he had written: "Lord, my heart is not haughty, nor mine eyes lofty; neither do I exercise myself in great matters, or in things too high for me" (Ps. 131:1 KJV). Wouldn't he now say, "Lord, You know me. You know I did not do that for myself. I did it because of my joy in having You as my God, and because You made me king. My heart was not haughty, was it? My eyes were not raised too high, were they?"

From that scene we turn to another scene in an upper room in Jerusalem some centuries later when the Son of David, who entered Jerusalem a few days before, was preparing to eat His last meal with His disciples. We have these words recorded: "Jesus, knowing that the Father had given all things into His hands, and that He had come from God and was going to God, rose from supper, laid aside His garments, and girded Himself with a towel. Then He poured water into a basin, and began to wash the disciples' feet and to wipe them with the towel with which He was girded" (John 13:3–5).

Here, then, were two kings. David, who was anointed king by a prophet, and the Son of David, who knew that God had put all things into His hands. Both were conscious that they were kings chosen by God, and as kings they decided to serve God in their own way. David danced, Christ washed feet! Both humbled themselves before God in an act that seemed ridiculous to the world. But because they were doing it for God, it was just between them and their God, and no one else mattered. When David danced before God, he said: "Lord, my heart is not lifted up; my eyes are not raised too high" (Ps. 131:1). When Christ washed the feet of His disciples, He also said: "Lord, my heart is not lifted up; My eyes are not raised too high."

When someone is able to say that, whether king or peasant, then he can also say what the rest of the psalm says: "Surely I have behaved and quieted myself, as a child that is weaned of his mother; my soul is even as a weaned child" (Ps. 131:2 KJV). When Spurgeon writes the desciption of this psalm in his "Treasury of David," he makes much of the weaned child, and he translates that verse like this: "Like a child who is weaned rests quietly at his mother's breast, so is my soul quieted within me." That makes this passage mean so much more. Here is a child who is no longer nursing. It is weaned. It is of an age when it no longer needs its mother's milk. But the mother still holds that child, and rocks that child, and presses it close to her breast . . . not to feed the child, but just to cuddle it and love it. That child no longer goes to the lap of the mother to be fed, but it goes to the mother's lap to be loved. So the child is quieted, not by being fed but by being loved.

It is strange what we remember about our childhood. As my mind goes back to my childhood, I can remember only one thing that took place in my life before I was five years old. I can remember only that I used to wait every evening for my mother to finish her work and come into the living room and sit in her rocking chair. There I would climb up in her lap and go to sleep, and I would never remember going to bed. I would wake up in the morning in my own room in my own bed. At that time I did not know why I did that every night. But now I know why it was so important for me. I wanted the security of being loved! Like a weaned child who is quieted at its mother's breast, so my soul is quieted. I am quieted by being loved by God, not because He feeds me but because He loves me.

Yes, David, you were a great king. But great as you were, you knew what you needed more than anything else—exactly what everybody else needs. You needed to be loved by your God! So you did not lift your heart up, you did not dare raise your eyes too high, because you needed God, for you yourself once said that there are two things which the Lord "will not endure": "haughty eyes and a proud heart" (Ps. 101:5 NIV).

So David was quieted as a weaned child is quieted at the breast of its mother. But the Son of David, it was not for Him! It was for His children, but it was not for Him! He was that Lord who would have to quiet His children. We see that in the garden that fateful night. Jesus went into the garden seeking to be quieted by His Father, but His Father was not there. God had forsaken Him! He had become sin that night for us, and His own Father turned away from Him because He had become sin, and God hates sin! So out into the garden He went alone. There He cried out: "Abba, Father . . . remove this cup from Me." Then He paced back and forth and threw Himself on the ground crying out again: "Father . . . remove this cup from Me; yet not what I will, but what Thou wilt." A third time He went out alone and said: "Father . . . remove this cup from Me; nevertheless not My will, but Thine, be done" (Mark 14:36; Luke 22:42).

Jesus had become a little child again in that garden, calling out to His Father. And although the Father sent an angel to strengthen Him, still Jesus had to tread that winepress alone.

The next day He went to that cross alone too, so that He could become that Parent to whom we can go and climb up in His lap and be quieted, and as a mother stills the heart of her weaned child, so Christ stills my heart.

Maundy Thursday

Unity, the Great Source of Blessing

The pilgrims have now arrived at their destination. The ascent to the Holy City is ended, and the business for which they came is about to begin. The pilgrims were together in the city to celebrate the Passover after the long and strenuous journey. Jesus was also there with His disciples in an upper room, eating their last meal together.

They have arrived. It is time to think about why they have been so blessed, and what will permit God to bless them even more. Christians must think of this often. Why has God so blessed us? Why has He called us to be His own and to live under Him in His kingdom? Ah yes, we have been blessed! God's own Son has been sent into this world to save the world. We can never measure the depth of the love which caused Christ's coming. We have received His grace. What blessings there are available to those who love His appearing! But now, as we converse with one another in the fellowship of this grace, what do we say to each other? As believers come together to speak of the blessings we have received and will receive out of the bounty of the grace of God in Christ, what do we talk about? What do we think about in those times of fellowship together?

Psalm 133, one of the last Psalms of Ascent, is just right for such an occasion when we are together discussing the blessings of God. Listen to it: "Behold, how good and pleasant it is when brothers dwell in unity! It is like the precious oil upon the head, running down upon the beard, upon the beard of Aaron, running down on the collar of his robes! It is like the dew of Hermon, which falls on the mountains of Zion! For there the Lord has commanded the blessing, life for evermore" (Ps. 133:1-3). When David wrote it, it was for his people. When Jesus recited it and sang it together with the male voices of His disciples, it was for His disciples: "Behold, how good and pleasant it is when brothers dwell in unity!"

"Behold!" Look at it! It is a wonder seldom seen! Just look at it . . . "how good and pleasant it is when brothers dwell in unity!" How much better it is than anything else. Just feel it! It is the best and the most pleasant experience in the world. Just look into your own heart and into your own experience and see if it isn't true that the best and most pleasant experiences you have ever had were when you experienced love and unity with another person.

How much better it was when Joseph revealed himself to his brothers there in Egypt years after they had sold him into slavery. How good and pleasant it was when they hugged and kissed one another and wept in happiness together in unity. How much better that was than when they dumped him into a pit to kill him! How much more pleasant it is for a congregation or a family to get along than when it is divided. Look at it! Behold! How much better it is to dwell together in unity. How good and pleasant it is! Why, of all things, would anyone want it any other way?

I will tell you what it is like, says David. "It is like the precious ointment upon the head, that ran down upon the beard, even Aaron's beard; that went down to the skirts of his garments" (KJV). That may not sound very meaningful at first reading, but every Israelite knew what it meant. It meant that Aaron was chosen for special blessings. When Aaron was chosen to be the high priest of Israel when Moses led the people out of bondage, they anointed Aaron with precious perfume and oil. It was the symbol of the fact that God had chosen him and that God would pour out special blessings upon Aaron. In order to prove to Aaron that the Lord would bless him immensely, they did not put just a few drops of the precious ointment on him. They poured it over his head! It is said that there were gallons of this ointment poured over his head, so that it ran down over his beard, down his garments, through the tassels at the bottom of the garments, and onto the floor. Man, when he was anointed, he was anointed! It was to show that when he was blessed by God, he was blessed! How good and pleasant it is to feel that kind of blessing poured out upon oneself or a fellow child of God. That is why David could say: "The Lord has commanded the blessing."

But not only that. It is even more pleasant than that, he says. It is like the dew of Mt. Hermon, like the dew that descends on the mountains of Zion. That is how the Lord has commanded His blessings!

A diary was found of a British army officer who was stationed in Palestine many years ago and wrote of his experience there beside Mt. Hermon. He said that Mt. Hermon is not like other mountains in the world which gradually rise up from lofty mountain plains. That mountain, he said, sits on flat land and rises nearly straight up from those tablelands to a height of over 10,000 feet. How amazed, he said, he was his first night there. It had been such a hot, parched day, as were all the days there. But then toward evening something astounding happened. There was suddenly a very cool breeze which sprang up, and the dew began to fall very heavily. He looked up to see what was happening, and there it was! The dew from Mt. Hermon! A warm breeze and the tropical sun had caught the snow-capped mountain and brought the cooling dew down to the tablelands until the tents and even the floors of the tents were wet. Now he understood why this land, which seemed a land of drought, could be covered with gardens and orchards and fertile crops. Now he knew what David meant: "How good and pleasant it is when brothers dwell in unity! It is like the dew of Hermon, which falls on the mountains of Zion!"

Ah yes, how good and pleasant it is when brothers dwell together in unity, for it is then that the Lord blesses them. Oh, forgive me! That is not what it says. It says that there the Lord *commands* His blessings! What a fascinating thought! Where there is unity among us, there the Lord commands His blessings to come to us; and where there is not unity, there God withholds blessings. We know that to be true. Think of it! If there is one way that we can call the blessings of God to us, this is it . . . that we love one another and that there be unity among us.

Of course, we know that God does what He wants to do, and for us to stand here and ask God to bless us in particular ways . . . well, God will do it if it pleases Him and if it is good for us. But if there is ever a time when we desperately need and want God's blessings to be poured on us like that oil and perfume was poured over the head of Aaron, running down his beard and over his clothing and onto the floor, then we must love one another and find unity in one another. Then, if it fits into His gracious plan for our life, God will command His blessings to come.

We have all watched congregations disintegrate. They have split, and half the congregation is asking the pastor to resign. Or people leave the congregation to join another, or they just don't attend the services. Those congregations have difficulty because the unity is gone, and it becomes quite obvious that the blessings of the Lord are withheld. Everything goes wrong. Nothing goes right. Few blessings are available to people who are not living in unity.

We have found this to be true also of a nation. If it is divided, blessings are few. When President Lyndon Johnson went before a national television audience some years ago and said he would not seek another term as president because the nation was divided, he was concerned that blessings would depart from us if we could find no way to live in unity. When Abraham Lincoln stood before this nation and quoted the saying of Jesus that a house divided against itself cannot stand, he was simply saying that a divided nation loses its blessings. It is a law of life which the Lord has enacted, that He commands His blessings to those who are united in love, and He withholds His blessings from those who are not united.

That is true even in family life. When a family does not get along, or the husband and wife are constantly bickering, not only does that family break up, but everything else goes wrong. The children go bad. There is more sickness in the family. Very often there is poverty and want. When a family does not live in love and unity, nothing else seems to go right. Again, the Lord withholds His blessings from those who do not dwell together in love and unity, but He commands His blessings to those who dwell together in unity.

Jesus knew this. That is why, on the last night of His earthly life, He gathered His disciples together to talk with them and eat His last meal with them. He knew He was about to die, and at a time like that, there is no time for anything except what is most important. If I knew I would die tomorrow, I would call my children together and speak to them about the most important things I know and about what I would want to leave them. There would be no time for anything else. Let me then paraphrase what Jesus said to His beloved disciples that night as John records it in his gospel.

"I am going away," Jesus said, "and where I am going you cannot come. But I will not leave you desolate, because I will send to you My Spirit and He will convince you of all the things that I have said to you. But first, I have something to say to you: 'Little children, love one another.' " Then He went on to say: "I am the vine, you are the branches. Every branch of Mine that does not bear fruit the father will take away. If a man does not abide in Me, he will be cast forth as a branch to wither. But again, I want to say something to you. A new commandment I give to you, that you love one another. I demand that you love one another! You are My friends if you do what I command you, that you love one another."

That was one of the few demands and commands that Jesus ever gave to His disciples . . . the command to love one another. He then went on to tell them about the blessings which would be theirs when the Comforter would come. But those blessings were always connected with His exhortation to them to love one another. He then ate His last meal with them, and after supper He passed out bread and wine, telling them that this was His body and blood, which He called "the new covenant . . . for the forgiveness of sins." But this too was connected with His exhortation to love one another so that they could have unity in sharing the body and blood of their Savior. Later in the church this Supper which the Christians shared together in the name of Christ began being called the "Love Feast," for it was their way of expressing and sharing their love with one another in unity.

After supper, that spring evening, Jesus went out into the garden to pray, and one thought still seemed to be uppermost in His mind . . . the unity and love of the disciples for each other. He wrestled in prayer for that unity as He said to His Father: "The glory which Thou hast given Me I have given to them, that they may be one even as We are one, I in them and Thou in Me, that they may become perfectly one" (John 17:22-23). He was still praying for their unity and love even to the end.

There were many other things that occurred between Jesus and His disciples that night, but one thing stands out above the rest. They were to love one another so that God could bless them and the work they were about to be called upon to do. That seemed to be the greatest concern of Jesus that last night of His earthly life . . . that His disciples love one another, for He knew that without love so little could be accomplished.

He, of course, knew that the disciples would never love perfectly. In fact, that is why He had to suffer and die—so that they, and we, could have forgiveness. But He also knew that the enterprise which He had begun—the building of His holy Christian church—would never fail, because He would send His Spirit to them. But He was concerned that with insufficient love the whole thing would be slowed down and curtailed. Without love there are so few blessings.

But where there is love . . . ah, look at it! Behold! There the Lord commands His blessings! Everything then moves ahead so well. Why would anyone want it any other way?

Good Friday

The Swearing of an Oath

When we are aware of the presence of the Lord, one of the things we do is make promises. We make those promises because we feel we should, although many times they are made simply for the purpose of trying to impress the Lord. People often utter oaths to the Lord, sometimes seriously, sometimes flippantly. Scripture always impresses upon us that an oath is terribly serious. It is that to God, so it must be also for us.

The pilgrims are now about to enter the Holy City to worship their God, and they are thinking about how they have lived since last they entered that holy place, and are about to renew their promises and oaths again. The seriousness of this matter is made fresh again as they remember other covenants and oaths made with their God. Psalm 132 reminds them of oaths to be made again, for David had made such oaths, and he always tried to keep them.

One of the major desires of David's life was to build the temple for the Lord, but it was the one thing he was not permitted to do. But that thought was always first and foremost in his mind. He always had wanted to find a place where the Lord could dwell in Israel. No wonder the Lord referred to David as a man after His own heart!

Psalm 132 describes this yearning of David when he says: "Remember, O Lord, in David's favor, all the hardships he endured; how he swore to the Lord and vowed to the Mighty One of Jacob, 'I will not enter my house or get into my bed; I will not give sleep to my eyes or slumber to my eyelids, until I find a place for the Lord, a dwelling place for the Mighty One of Jacob' " (Ps. 132:1-5).

Having made that vow, that before he went into his own house, to his own bed, he would first find a place for the Lord's house, it was now time for David to fulfill it. David was not permitted to build that temple, but he was allowed to find the place where it would be built. The time had now come for him to fulfill that vow to find such a place. A vow was not something that one took lightly in those days. The great patriarchs of old seldom made a vow, because they knew the consequences if it was not fulfilled. And if they ever did make a vow, they were certain to fulfill it, for that was a promise made to the Lord. They would rather die than break a vow.

David now had to fulfill that vow because he had just finished building his palace. It was a magnificent building. The Pharaohs of Egpyt would have been proud of it. But now David would not live in it. He would not live in his own house, nor sleep in his own bed, until his vow was performed, to find a place where the temple of God would be built. So he neither had his palace blessed, nor did he live in it.

His problem was that he could not find a suitable place for the temple to be built, for the Lord had not yet revealed it to him. So he did the next best thing. He decided that he would bring the Ark of the Covenant into Jerusalem and set up a tent for it, and he began preparations to bring it there.

But where was it? No one seemed to know. It had been put away and hidden because it brought so much devastation to that nation when they sinned. Then David remembered something from his childhood days, for he says in this psalm that while he lived in Bethlehem some rumors used to float around that little town that the ark was in a woods near Bethlehem. So he had some men look for it there, and sure enough they found it.

Out they went into the woods to bring it in. They put it on an oxcart, with the Levites in charge of bringing it in. Everything was ready! The grand procession began! But then something happened! The oxen stumbled, and one of the Levites reached out to steady the ark. The record states that the Lord was angry with the man who touched the ark and struck him dead.

With that, the procession stopped and everything became very silent. David did not know what to do, but it states that he became very angry that the Lord should have killed his good friend the Levite for trying to save the ark. But he was not only angry; he was afraid too. So he decided to give up his wish of bringing the ark into Jerusalem that day. Everyone went back to their homes in silence and frustration, and the ark was left there in the home of a man.

After three months the news reached David that that man was being greatly blessed, so he knew the Lord was no longer angry, and he decided to try it again. The preparations were again made to bring that ark into the city. This time, however, it was done much more carefully and solemnly, for they now realized that this was not David's procession. It was the Lord's! This time it went as they planned, with this difference: This time it became an awesome event, a frightening one. This time they made their preparations with deep reverence. They sensed that they had God in their hands, so it had better be done very carefully.

That may seem like a long introduction to this Psalm 132, but without that background it would be hard for us to understand the full meaning of this psalm, as they sang: "Remember, O Lord, in David's favor, all the hardships he endured; how he swore to the Lord and vowed to the Mighty One of Jacob, 'I will not enter my house or get into my bed; I will not give sleep to my eyes or slumber to my eyelids, until I find a place for the Lord, a dwelling place for the Mighty One of Jacob' " (Ps. 132:1-5). This was now a frightening moment for them, and all was not jolly now. They had learned something that day . . . that when you handle sacred things, you handle them with the deepest of respect and awe and wonder.

Knowing this, then, about our God, that He demands and requires such respect that even to mistakenly handle Him brings about dire consequences, it is even more amazing what He then permitted men to do to Him when He visited this earth in person. Here was Jesus, Very God of Very God Himself, coming into this world. The fulness of the Godhead dwelt in Him bodily, and He put Himself into the hands of men.

And here is what they did to Him: They ridiculed Him, they spat on Him, they crowned Him with thorns, they beat Him with rods, they whipped Him, and then they threw Him down on a cross and nailed His body to it and set it in a hole and made Him die there. And He took it! Never did He lift a finger against them! Why? Our psalm tells us why. Because God had made a vow. He had taken an oath. He had sworn to David, and He would not turn from it! He swore He would save His people, and He had chosen Zion and Jerusalem from which to reign.

When a man makes a vow to God, he had better keep it; but when God makes a vow, it is a foregone conclusion that it will be kept! God's most potent weapon is His own Word. The psalm says: "The Lord swore to David a sure oath from which He will not turn back: 'One of the sons of your body I will set on your throne' " (Ps. 132:11). Why did He take it? Because He had sworn an oath . . . the oath to establish the throne of David forever. He had sworn it, so He would do it! So He took all of this in His Son, the Son of David, so that He could save His people and set up the throne of David forever.

Who were these people who put Him to death? Why, they were the governing council, children of David's line! He could not destroy them because He had taken an oath. Whose temple was this that refused Him? It was, so to speak, David's temple, built from the desire of his heart. Who was sitting in judgment upon Him? It was David's priest and David's temple! Whose people were these who shouted, "Crucify Him!"? They were David's people!

God had taken an oath, that David's royal line, that David's temple, that David's people would be saved. So He took it all for the sake of David. When Solomon, David's son, went bad and married a thousand wives, and worshiped the gods of those thousand wives, the Lord said He would not punish Solomon, for the sake of David. When Assyria later attacked Jerusalem, the Lord told King Hezekiah that He would not permit Assyria to waste one Jewish life, He would not permit one arrow to fly into the city, He would not permit a lengthy siege. Why? Because of His servant David, a man after His own heart. The Lord had taken a vow, and no man was going to make the Lord break that vow.

Peter used that as his argument when he stood up in that crowd on Pentecost and said to them that this Jesus whom they crucified was the Christ, the Son of David. He said: "Men and brethren, let me freely speak unto you of the patriarch David, that he is both dead and buried, and his sepulchre is with us unto this day. Therefore being a prophet, and knowing that *God had sworn with an oath to him,* that of the fruit of his loins, according to the flesh, he would raise up Christ to sit on his throne" (Acts 2:29-30 KJV) . . . therefore He brought Him back from the dead.

God had taken an oath! That is why He took it all in spite of how they handled Him, because He had taken an oath! This is why we say with Paul: "He must reign until He has put all His enemies under His feet" (1 Cor. 15:25), for this is that Son of David to whom God swore an oath that He would reign forever and ever.

This God of David is our God! When David says that God swore by an oath that He had chosen Zion to be His habitation, this is the God who has chosen us who have received Jesus as that

Son of David, and He has chosen us with an oath. He has said it this way: Whosoever believes in Jesus Christ shall be saved (cf. John 3:16). When we think of the abuse God took from those people when they crucified Him, because He swore to it, how much more can we have confidence in this God who swore to save those who believe in Jesus Christ! For if an entire nation and race was saved for David's sake, how much more are we saved for Christ's sake, we who are of His own nation, as Peter said: "You are a chosen race, a royal priesthood, a holy nation" (1 Peter 2:9). I don't know about you, but I can live in that confidence, because when my God has sworn an oath, I believe it!

Thomas Fuller tells of how he satisfied a lifelong desire of his by rowing down to London on the Thames River. He explained that above London that river winds and meanders and loiters in all directions. It doesn't seem to know where it wants to go. It seems to have no destination. It meanders 100 miles by water over a stretch that is only 20 miles by land. But once it reaches London, it seems to know where it is going. Straight to the sea it goes! Twenty miles by water, twenty miles by land! In London it discovers where it is going.

It is at the foot of the cross as I watch my Savior bleed and die that I discover where I am going. He is bleeding and dying because of an oath which His Father made concerning my eternal salvation. He promised that a Seed would be born of a woman one day who would crush the head of the serpent. He promised that He would be of Abraham's seed, of the tribe of Judah, of the line of David, and that He would be a Suffering Servant before whom we would hide our faces. I find Him hanging there on a cross, dying for my sins. When I come to that cross, I know where I am going. If it has cost the Lord that much to fulfill His oath to me, then straight to heaven will I go. It is at the cross, where the Lord's oath was fulfilled, that I know where I am going.

Contrapuntal Dialogs
for Lent

by Frederick W. Kemper

Foreword

Dialog sermons can move in several different ways. Predetermined questions can be met with standard answers. Youth can meet age, naiveté can meet experience. The dialog's course can be determined by an attempt to get into the psyche of the characters, real or imagined.

The dialogs presented in this little volume are "contrapuntal." That is, Jesus talks and several of the people of the passion talk, but they do not talk to each other. Jesus starts from a point of His experience with the character; the character usually starts from where he is at the moment. The two speak independently of each other. At one point in the dialog they meet for a moment, then move on, each in his own thought direction.

Original presentation of the dialogs was from the pulpit and lectern. "Jesus" occupied the pulpit. The introductory remarks, setting the scene for the dialog and providing a touch of background material, although printed in the Order for Worship, were read. The dialog began. Many people felt the characters might have been closer, say at reading desks, to avoid the tennis match effect. The readers faced the congregation at all times, reading and conducting themselves as if the other didn't exist. Some thought was given to costuming; then the whole idea was discarded when Satan turned up.

It seemed permissible to make "Jesus" speak. It is one of the joys of the faith that He and we identify with each other. The Father would not "speak." That is why the angel, standing somewhere near, is on hand in the sixth dialog. The angels saw what was going on down there on the cross and they could see the Father in His agony. They must speak among themselves sometimes about the redemption even now; and when the conversation is done, they sing a little louder and a bit more joyously, for the grace of the Lord never ceases to amaze them.

F.W.K.

1

Simon and His Lord

An Introduction

The place is imaginary; the time is indeterminate; the privilege is poetic; the purpose is to look into the heart of Jesus.

Let's place Simon Peter, the Rock, in a lower-level dungeon not far from the Forum in Rome. He is in chains. He is there in our thinking pattern tonight only because we want him to rethink his life out loud, and he couldn't do that unless he were near the end of it. In fact, tomorrow they will crucify him. His last request will be to hang head down on his cross, for he was unworthy, he said, to die as had his Master.

Think Jesus where you will . . . in the prison cell with Simon, high on a lofty throne with cherubim about Him . . . it doesn't matter, for just as 1,000 years are as a moment, so 1,000 miles are but a touch away with our Lord.

Peter speaks.

The Dialog

Peter
I feel in my whole being
    that the end is not far off.
Last month they allowed me visitors.
Silvanus was here. . . .
    I hope he was able to take my letter
    to all those living in the dispersion,
    to give them comfort and strength
    in the provident purposes of God,
        should their loyalty and love for Jesus
        bring them to imprisonment or to death.
No visitor for these two weeks.
The guards are sullen and silent.
I am quite certain that my end is near.

Jesus,
    I am not worried . . . not about myself.
You died, and death became a shadow to be desired
    as departure here
    and as arrival at the mansions.
I saw Your grave with John that day,
    empty save for angel heralds of good news.

I talked with You. . . .
        You asked me if I loved You,
                early one bright morning
                on the sands of Galilee.
        Nurse My lambs, You said,
        and feed My sheep.
No, I am not worried about myself,
        but Jesus, Lamb of God,
                the sheep in persecution—
        I worry over them.
I commend them to Your loving care.
I pray,
        I pray that I have fed them well.
                My back is breaking,
                        for these short chains
                        do not allow me room to stand.
                        Cold and pain shoot through my being.
                My wrists are raw and bleeding from these
                        iron links.
                The silence! Will no one speak to me?
                The rats,
                        the creeping things,
                        the filth!
                The silence. What do you do with silence?
                        For now . . . for now . . . I think I go afishing
                        once again.
                        Not for fish—but for remembering.

I remember how it was,
        late in the day . . . the sun still hot,
        the shadows long . . . and the air still, so still.
I cannot understand, not even now, why He picked me
        to be one of the favored twelve, nor yet
        one of the favored three.
                I was loud in those days.
                I said my piece, letting hurt fall where it would.
                I had no patience with people,
                        and little with life.
                I never went to rabbinical school.
                I couldn't even write my name.
                I stank of fish.

Jesus
How does a man go about choosing disciples,

twelve true and tested men?
Book learning? Personality?
A battery of tests? Lengthy interviews?
References and a cross check of his past?
I knew the kind of man My Simon was.
Blustery like an autumn day, blowy like a March wind.
I knew he was a fisherman,
    like half the townsmen near the sea.
I knew he was illiterate.
But Simon had a capacity for loyalty. . . .
    I needed loyal men to stand beside Me.
He learned quite slowly, that I knew,
    but learn he could.
And I knew the power of the Spirit,
    who could take a man like Simon
    and make a bulwark,
        a rock,
        a fortress, out of him.
That's why I called him Peter.
    Peter—the Rock,
        that's what he could and would become
        before our days together ended.
Yes, Simon, the ROCK, was a good choice.

Peter

He said, "Follow Me!"
It was as simple as that . . .
    and life was changed forever.
It took some courage, I remember.
    Fishing, I had income
        and food on my table.
    Not much future in fishing,
        but a lot of security.
Then He said, "Follow Me!"
And I did.

He sent us out once on a trial run.
Two by two we went
    from home to home,
    from village to village.
We had power from Jehovah
    to heal the sick,
        to cast out devils,
            to raise the dead!
It was a baptism with fire,

an awesome responsibility
to have power like that.
We tried to be His men . . .
we spoke of the kingdom of the living God
and told, at each encounter,
of the Nazarene.
Some people loved us
and listened to our story of the Christ.
Others turned against us,
and I first tasted persecution.
I almost quit.
I almost told Him to keep His kingdom
before that internship was over.

Jesus
I have always sought to be compassionate.
Blind men have beheld the skies,
and lame men have skipped again at My command,
and sorrowing hearts have leaped for joy
at some healing or revivification.
I have known the future, too.
I knew well the problems loyal men
would one day face for Me,
when they went on missions in My name.
I knew well enough My servant Paul
would die, his head upon the block;
that Bartholomew would be flayed and Peter crucified;
that James would be thrown
from the dizzying heights of Zion
at the very place where once Satan bid Me leap.
Always I have sought to help My people
know that I am near,
to know My strength in human weakness. . . .
Then,
should greater trials come,
their victory would have been won
already in the lesser trial.
Peter needed the crucible
first with lower heat and easy experience,
that he might better survive the greater heat
when at last it came.

Peter
He called me "Satan" once.

I will never forget that!
He said I was Satan.
"Get behind Me, Satan!"
     Those were His very words to me.
I was sitting on a rock at our wilderness retreat.
That's funny, "the Rock" sitting on a rock.
The question of His identity was at stake.
I thought I knew Him well by then.
When He asked the question, I had the answer.
"You are the Christ, the Son of the living God,"
     I told Him.
The trouble then was,
     I didn't know
     what it meant to be "the Christ,"
     nor yet to be "the Son of the living God."
And when He said
     He had to go to Jerusalem
     to be lifted on a torturous cross . . .
     when He said He had to die . . .
          "Not You, Lord. Not You," I cried at Him.
Think a moment.
     He was the very focal point of every virtue . . .
          kindness—who was ever kinder than He . . .
          graciousness—who ever lived with grace surpassing His . . .
          mercy—who loved the sinner more than He . . .
          love—we never truly understood that word until
               He showed us what it means.
     He was the embodiment of the very power of God . . .
          lame men walked at His command,
          and lifeless children laughed again,
          and Malchus got back the ear I severed.
          He prayed forgiveness for the brutal soldiers
               who fixed Him to His cross.
     But I didn't understand Him.
          His kindness and His mercy and His love
               reached their ultimate on Golgotha,
          and the greatest miracle of all—
               the most Godlike act He performed—
          was to die for all humanity.
No—out there in Caesarea Philippi
     I didn't understand . . . not yet.

Jesus
To love is not easily willed, not really.

Sometimes it means to watch
    My beloved ones get hurt
        (for ofttimes the hurting
        is more helpful than the soothing).
And sometimes it means to hurt a little,
    for the lesson must be learned
    against the bigger hurt.
Poor, dear Rock . . . great, good Rock.
My great big talk-and-act man!
It took him so long to understand.
I don't suppose if Pentecost
    had not been in the decision for salvation
    he ever would have grasped the whole great plan.

Peter

There was the time He washed our feet
    when we gathered to celebrate
    the ancient feast
        at His desire.

Jesus

How slowly they learned
        the lessons of love and service,
    My men—
        arguing about greatness and greatest
        and who will sit where in the Kingdom.
The great pendulum was swinging . . .
    the hour would strike before the sun went down.
They had to understand . . .
    every man is servant to every other.
    I came to serve, not be served;
    I ask the same of all My people.

That night, with patience and love,
    and ministering and kindness
        all at stake,
    I took basin and towel
        and one by one I washed
        their tired, dusty feet.
    James and John, sons of thunder, with their
        volatile tempers and faster tongues . . .
            I washed their feet.
    Judas, with the churning mind and pounding heart,
        was tense beyond control
        when I knelt before him and slowly

68

      washed and dried his feet.
Gentle Nathanael, refined, learned,
        quiet Nathanael,
    said no word to Me,
    but I knew the act perplexed him
    and that he would search for meaning in it.
Thomas muttered his Thomas kind of muttering,
    about not believing what he was seeing.
    But his muttering only helped Me to know
    it mattered that I cool and wipe his feet.
Matthew was most gracious.
    I did not look at him,
    for My love must be in My deed,
      not My eyes,
    even for this man who needed love so
      desperately.
Peter, then, thought he knew his place
    and sought to tell Me
    with his boisterous protestation
    that he saw no need for Me to wash his feet;
    with him the issues ran deep
    and he had to understand the washing
    still to come before the sun went down
      a second time.
Then Andrew,
    Thaddeus,
    Philip of the loaves and fishes,
    the other James,
    and the Simon from
    the land of Canaan.

                                  (Pause)

Peter. Peter! Don't remember that!

Peter
He told me! He told me I would deny Him.
"Not me, Lord. I'll defend You to the death!"
And there I was at the fire in the courtyard. . . .
    A pretty little servant girl,
    quite naive and very gentle,
    excited to see a face she knew,
    and wanting to be noticed for remembering
      —she recognized me.
Her soft voice, her gentle words,

seemed screaming sirens to me.
She had found my secret and revealed it.
She had, in innocence, implicated me
   in what was going on inside.
I took an oath.
     "By God," I said. "By almighty God,
        I do not know the Man," I said.

Jesus
They were moving Me through the courtyard.
The Sanhedrin had been called.
   My trial was about to begin.
The cock was crowing.
   I could see the cock, proud
     against the first light of dawn.
   And hear him. . . .
     Once he crowed,
     then twice, then
     yet once again.
I had to catch Peter's eye.
He had to know I loved him,
   that I understood,
   that I did not hold his rashness
     damning to his soul.
I had to help him know that in a little while,
   when the cross was finished,
     every sin would be covered and forgiven.

Peter
When it was over, I cried.
What a travesty of my devotion to Him.
What kind of a friend was I?
I am glad He looked at me,
   that I saw what I did in His eyes.
   Had He not passed by at the very moment,
     with that look of love and forgiveness,
   I might have joined Judas in deep remorse
     and dark despair.

Then the crucifixion!
I watched from a distance—
   terrified,
     panic-stricken,
        desolate.
I was stunned.

I recall the day's ending only with difficulty,
  even now.
      The still, cool body, down from the cross.
      The burial, the stone, the guard.
And through it all the unbelievable fear
  that we might be next . . .
  and a gathering of the group,
      and locked doors.

Jesus
They didn't understand.
I told them a thousand times.
  They didn't understand.
I said it in a hundred different ways.
  They didn't understand.
Neither then nor now do I fault
  a single one of them.
Only let the Spirit touch them
  and they will know and believe.

Peter
Mary brought the news.
John and I ran to the tomb.
  It was empty.
I heard angels talking.
  I took the winding sheet in my hand.
Bewilderment followed bewilderment.
"He is risen!" Indeed!

Jesus,
  we saw You.
  We saw Your wounds.
  We heard Your voice.
  We broke bread with You.
  You asked me, "Do you love Me?" . . .
      And I wasn't really sure,
      not then.

Jesus
The Plan. The Plan.
I wanted then and there
  to bless them all with the Holy Spirit.
But the Plan—said—wait.
I would have gotten on with it.
The Plan said fifty days . . .
  then the Holy Spirit

would have His day.

Peter
Pentecost!
   That was the day.
Sounds of furious winds and dancing flames . . .
   and the Holy Spirit came to us.
This little old fisherman got up
   and preached his first sermon.
Everything was righted;
   from that moment on
         no man,
         no government,
         no prison,
         no death
            would sway me from my devotion
            to the Christ.

Jesus
I was proud of Peter, the Rock.
I was there when he spoke at Pentecost;
   I saw him change
         into a man on fire for My kingdom.
   I watched him in prison that first time,
         and how he spoke to the guards
         and at the trial to his accusers.
   I know where he is even now,
         suffering for My name's sake.

Peter
Dawn has come; I hear the prison guard
   is changing watch.
The change seems longer than routine.
Why are they taking so long this morning?
      Ah. My back is fairly broken with this pain.
      These leg irons are short, and wear against
         my flesh.
      I am thirsty.
         Will no one bring me water?
The voices grow louder.
      Yet I cannot make them out.
Jesus. Jesus!
It is quiet again!
No. No.
      There are soldiers on the steps.

Do You hear me, Jesus?
    Help me to be strong.
    Be patient with me, Jesus.
    Keep me faithful to the end.
Jesus! Jesus!

                                        Amen.

2

Caiaphas and the Christ

An Introduction

Whatever happened to Caiaphas? Except for his appointment by the Roman governor Quirinius in A.D. 18 to the office of high priest in the temple at Jerusalem, a post which he held for 18 years, nothing would be known of him, were it not for his encounter with Jesus.

St. John informs us that the raising of Lazarus triggered an enormous determination in Caiaphas to be rid of Jesus; St. Matthew adds the significant point that it was "for envy" that Caiaphas delivered Jesus to Pilate for execution.

It would be interesting to hear Caiaphas' story. The feeling comes immediately that that story, too, has two sides. That is what is proposed for the meditation this evening—a brief examination of the two sides of a fantastic encounter.

Using a great deal of poetic license, as much imagination as the method of presentation will allow, but above all using the facts and interpretations of the encounter as honestly as possible, the stories might resolve something like this dialog.

Caiaphas sits in his splendid mansion on Mount Zion, Jerusalem. Few people visit him any longer. He is a broken man. What he thought would be his moment of glory has become his tragedy. Not that everyone followed the Nazarene; nobody found Caiaphas his man after that.

Jesus is speaking.

The Dialog

Jesus
When Moses stood before the burning bush,
 to meet My Father and to receive from Him
 the program for delivery of the slaves of Egypt,
 My Father, wanting him to understand
 that he stood in the holy presence of almighty God,
 bade him remove his sandals,
  for the very ground whereon he stood was sacred.
Whenever a man stands in the presence of God,
 let him remember to remove his shoes.
Sometimes I wonder if,
 in Our great councils,
 We did right or made a great mistake

in not resolving the problem of foreknowledge,
  and predestination and freedom of the will.
My people wrestle time and time again
  with the mighty dilemma with which We left them.
Somehow, in the midst of the story of My passion
  the dilemma reaches its most profound proportions.
  It spills over into
    the problems of day-to-day existence.
"Did Judas have to betray You in the Garden?" people ask.
"Did Caiaphas, and Herod, and poor Pontius Pilate
  have to act the way they did?"
"If the Holy Spirit inspired the prophecies
  written by the ancient prophets,
  did the passion have to take that course?"
By the rules of the game, I cannot answer them,
  for they must struggle and search for answers
    for themselves;
  We can do nothing to violate the faith factor . . .
  nothing to stop the searching.

Caiaphas is a case in point.
Knowing I am Lord of history,
    My people insist their questions.
  "Did You see to it that Quirinius was appointed
    by the emperor?"
  "Did You cause the encounter between him and Caiaphas
    and effect the appointment to the priestly office?"
  "Is Caiaphas a pawn in the divine chess game to be
    sacrificed to the common good?"
Questions like these, they ask;
  and I cannot give them answer.
    Not now.

Caiaphas
Eighteen years I served, only to come to this.
My father-in-law somehow lost favor with the Romans.
Ismael and Eleazar and Simeon
  had their chance at priesthood,
  but they were fools.
Then by chance we met these many years ago,
  Quirinius and I.
In that one brief encounter we understood each other.
  Before long I had the office
  with its power and income.

Life was good.
A little favor here and there,
    and Rome stayed satisfied.
As a Sadducee
    I had some problems with the Pharisees,
    but I knew how to smooth them over.
I kept things going in Herod's masterpiece on Zion.
    We observed the feasts and fasts,
    and daily offered sacrifice according to the
        ancient rituals.
    We accommodated tourists and pilgrims
        with hand-picked lambs.
    We made available doves for sacrifices for the poor.
    The incense burned unceasingly,
        its smoke spiraling to the heavens,
        symbol of our faith and prayers.
    With solemn awe I passed each year behind the veil
        to sprinkle blood upon the mercy seat.
The job paid well, let there be no misunderstanding that,
    but I was accustomed to gracious living . . .
    and needed more than most.

Then He turned up.
Reports from people on His doings came in.
    "He changed water into wine," they said.
    "He cured a fevered lad, a Gentile's son," they said.
    "He called a dead boy back to life," they said.
    "The crowds who hear Him grow larger," they said.
    "He talks against the faith," they said.
We began to be concerned.
At first it was nothing,
    but the crowds were getting larger.
I'll admit: I began to feel threatened.
We had committee meetings about it.
    Nothing we dreamed up in committee worked.
    He was more than a match for some of our best minds.
The straw that broke the camel's back was Lazarus.
    The day that news came
        I knew that He had gone too far.
What to do! What to do?
Then word came that He had marched right into the temple,
    my temple! and with unequaled gall upset
        the tables of the changers.
    Money rolled across the floor.

You can bet more found its way into beggars' pockets
        than ever was recovered.
He opened the sheep pens and the pigeon cages.
The pigeons were lost, and those stupid sheep panicked
        and bolted through the temple courts.
That's when I made up my mind about that Man.
He had to go for the common good.
Miracles, and crowds, and now this.
Only one course made sense.
        He must be removed once and for all.

Jesus
The Plan allowed three years
        to change the course of history
        and to change men's minds,
            which was undoubtedly the greater challenge.
Once the plan for man's salvation had been given impetus
        at the river's edge through Cousin John,
        no moment might be lost
        and every possible device to catch and hold
        the hearts of men must be employed.
Signs and wonders, more to catch the heart
            than hold the eye,
        and preaching calculated to seize attention
            and to change men's lives,
        and all the while living by the high ideals
            established by My Father.

The overriding factor was to fill the mansions of My Father,
        to populate eternity robbed of citizens by Adam's fall,
        to woo and win men with profoundest love to the covert
            of the Father's wings.
No man could be beyond the love
        proceeding from the heart of God.
I reached for Judas, betrayer, lest he become a son
            of eternal perdition,
        but he led the band of soldiers
            with their spears and staves,
        and gave identification with a kiss of peace.
            Ah, Judas, I weep for you.
And I strained with reaching for the heart of Caiaphas.

Caiaphas
There is a weak spot in every man's defenses.
Two days after the affair with the money changers

77

one Judas of Kerioth appeared and bargained
for a consideration to lead us to our quarry.
I am not above a little sarcasm.
I loathed the man who thus betrayed his Master,
so I haggled until the price was down to thirty pieces . . .
the price of a slave, though I doubt he realized it.
On Wednesday our quarry did not appear in Jerusalem.
On Thursday, shortly before sundown,
word arrived from our contact
that Gethsemane would be the place . . .
and to be ready with our soldiers
about the time of curfew.
Until we had Him safe in hand we could do nothing more.
When everything went according to schedule,
we brought our prize to the home of my wife's father.
I dispatched messengers
to announce a meeting of the Sanhedrin
and to find a few beggars to witness against Him—
for a sum.
Within the hour the Sanhedrin had gathered,
the witnesses had been found,
and I was committed beyond return to the course
I had determined.

Jesus
When I had finished praying in the garden
and learned that there was no recourse
in My Father's mind
to redeem the souls of men some other way . . .
when the messenger of heaven brought answer to My agony
by pointing to the cross . . .
I knew then I must expect no quarter.
Judas came to brush his lips against My cheek.
I loved Judas, but he would not understand
what it meant to know the Christ.
I saw him leave the garden,
and I longed to call to him:
Don't, Judas! Don't!
Did his hanging from that jutting limb
speak of his love for Me?
Then it was love without understanding.

They brought Me to the Sanhedrin,
there to face on their terms

the leaders of all Israel.
A face here and there I recognized.
    Nicodemus sat turned to the shadows
        that I might not see him.
Caiaphas was in charge,
    and ran the meeting with a leader's hand.
Here was My church, My beloved church,
        represented by these men,
    and on their faces, written almost on each one,
    was determination to find Me guilty of a crime
    of sufficient gravity to take My life.
My church! My people! Sheep of My Father's flock!
Judas first. Now this.

Caiaphas
There He stood. Jesus of Nazareth . . .
    as good as dead already,
    given half a chance to work my plan.
We went through the witnesses.
    The whole procedure was a farce;
    by the third perjurer there was no doubt about that.
We finally stayed within the letter of Sanhedrin law
    when two sniveling creatures accused Him of boasting
    that in three days He could rebuild my temple . . .
        Herod's temple.
Who did He think He was, God?
That's what I seized upon . . .
    this fellow says He is God.
The case was still weak;
    I could feel uneasiness in the room.
Then it came to me like a flash.
I'll make Him condemn Himself.
Controlling myself, I slowly stood up.
I looked at Him with the coldest eyes
    I have ever looked at anyone.
I slowly raised my hand to heaven.
Slowly and deliberately I did what we people of the covenant
    do not ever do.
        I demanded an oath of Him.
My words?
"I adjure You
    by the living God,
        tell us if You are the Christ,
            the Son of God."

Jesus
Most pointedly, when first I began My public ministry,
    I laid down the principles by which I lived.
You will find these points written in My biographies.
One of them pleaded for absolute honesty,
    for dealing invariably in truth.
"Let your communication be: Yea, yea; nay, nay;
    for whatsoever is more than these cometh of evil" (KJV)
Everything I said during My visit with mankind was spoken
    in the binding medium of that oath.
When Caiaphas adjured Me,
    when he demanded I answer under oath,
    I knew I would be speaking before him
    and all My accusers as I had never spoken before.
No other person asked Me to take oath
    to give credence to My message.
Caiaphas did.
        And in the answering to his question,
        under oath before the living God,
        before My beloved Father, if you will,
        I spoke the Gospel news with greater force
        than it has ever been spoken before or since.

Caiaphas
That did it.
That was the clincher in the whole business.
I saw Him wince when I asked the question.
He took His time answering, too.
There was no question in my mind about the outcome now,
    answer how He would.
It was a dramatic moment!
"I adjure You by the living God,
    tell us if You are the Christ, the Son of God."

Jesus
The horror of Caiaphas' demand haunts Me yet.
I could not believe that he was serious.
What he demanded was a public proclamation,
            under oath,
    of My Messiahship—in order to condemn Me.
While I had not hesitated
    to speak of Myself as the Messiah,
    I had avoided doing it in such a way
    that it would bring My condemnation

before the time set in the Plan.
Now that time had come.

Caiaphas
It was the masterstroke of the trial.
"I adjure You by the living God . . ."
It was my own idea, all the way;
     but then, that's why I was high priest.

Jesus
I was under Sanhedrin law.
My whole purpose as the Christ was at stake.
Caiaphas cut through to the central issue.
When I answered him,
     he could never say again
     that he had not been called by the Gospel
          to repentance and faith.

Caiaphas
"I adjure You by the living God . . ."

Jesus
Under oath, I looked long at him.
Then I said two words:
     "Thou sayest."
So, in a moment, in a word,
     I made My last pronouncement of the truth.
Caiaphas, take off your shoes.
The ground whereon you stand is holy.

Caiaphas
That was it.
The rest of the way, with a little careful engineering,
     would be downhill.
The councilmen voted "Yea" to the death sentence
     by an overwhelming majority.

Pilate was an early riser.
We could have the whole business done by noon.
As it was, we had the Nazarene on the cross
     by the third hour.
He was dead by the ninth hour.

I want you to know I acted in good faith.
I can't deny a certain jealousy. He was far too popular.
But the covenant people were at stake,
     and whatever else I might have been,

I had some concern for them.
He challenged our whole way of life.
He demanded changes in the faith.
No man can claim to be God
    and be allowed to live.

My days are long and lonely.
Every day I watch the walkway leading to this house of mine;
    no one comes.
Things started falling apart for me not long after that.
I hung in the priesthood for another year or two
    before I left.
The temple was never quite the same.
The rent veil—although we soon repaired it—
    bothered us more than we cared to admit.
And all that talk about Him
    having risen from the dead!
I'm a lonely, broken old man.
Jehovah God! What's to become of me?

Jesus
I often weep for Caiaphas.
But My tears do not stop with him,
    for countless others have stood
        on the same holy ground,
    have heard the proclamation of the truth,
    and in like manner have kept on their shoes
        in unbelief.

I hear the question once again:
    Did Caiaphas have to do the thing he did
    because My Father willed him to?
And I say again to all who ask it,
    Let faith leap beyond the question
        and grasp the cross,
    lest the lonely hour come and find you unprepared.
My yes is yes; My no, no.
I say it on that affirmation.
I am the Christ. The Son of the living God.
Take off your shoes.

                                    Amen.

Herod and John's Cousin

An Introduction

Edom (Idumea, Seir) lies in the wild, dry country south of the Dead Sea. When Esau, son of Isaac and brother of Jacob, left Canaan to find room for his cattle, he settled in the land of Mount Seir. "So Esau dwelt in the hill country of Seir; Esau is Edom" (Gen. 36:8). Esau is "the father of the Edomites" (Gen. 36:9).

A family from Edom by the name of Herod became rulers in Palestine from 37 B.C. to 70 A.D. Herod the Great, husband of 10 wives, father of many children, hosted the wise men and massacred the innocents of Bethlehem. Herod Antipas, a sly, crafty ruler, tetrarch or governor of Galilee and Perea, is the same who had John the Baptist beheaded and opposed Jesus. He was followed in A.D. 40 by Herod Agrippa, who killed James and imprisoned Paul. Finally, Herod Agrippa II became governor. It is before him and Festus, Roman governor of Judea, that Paul made his defense of the Christian faith.

Herod Antipas speaks in our dialog this evening. Undergirded with theology, searching behind the Luke account (only Luke records this portion of Jesus' trial), tying in references to Herod and Jesus, and using the poet's license, an imaginary dialog between Herod and Jesus, when in later years Herod was in exile in Gaul, might have gone like this.

Jesus speaks first.

The Dialog

Jesus
My ancestry has been carefully recorded
    in the sacred records.
The list includes names like Abraham, Isaac, and Jacob,
    whose primary claim to fame
    is their patriarchal position
    at the fountainhead of Jewish history.
Names like David and Solomon are in the list too.
But many of the names are shadows without substance.
The birthright, the privilege of being in My ancestry,
was carefully guarded by certain generations,
    while others thought it of no consequence.

Two millennia before My incarnation at Bethlehem,
    Esau, eldest son of Isaac,

a man of the woods and the wild,
who by all the tribal rights should have received
the blessing of his father and thereby be included
in My genealogies . . .
    went hunting.
While he was gone, Rebekah and Jacob conspired
    for the blessing from blind Isaac
and by deception and compounded lies
    managed to secure it.
Thus by lie and oath Jacob's name
    is entered in My genealogy,
    in place of Esau's.

Herod

These barren reaches of Gaul are a far cry from Galilee.
To be banished at the end of one's career
    by the lying charges of one's own nephew,
    is a most grievous culmination.
Why did I allow Agrippa breath? A word, and my soldiers
    would have run him through.
Think! That's all there is to do in this barren place.
Think, think, think!
Think ahead! Herodias says. To what, I ask . . . death?
Think back! My mind keeps reverting,
    to the great days when I had power,
    when I could scheme and manage
    to hold my place and secure the tetrarchy.
I think, and sometimes I am certain
    that thinking will drive me to despair.

Jesus

The struggle between Jacob and Esau
    was not easily resolved.
Esau flew into a rage that he had been deceived,
    and at the old man's urging
    Jacob fled to Paddan-aram, to his uncle's home.
My father, Joseph, used to tell Me of their struggle
    to find some kind of truce . . .
    how Jacob wrestled with the angel
    until his thigh was out of joint
    and how they came at last to reconciliation.
        Then Esau took his flocks to Edom,
            while Jacob struck his tent
            and made his home in Canaan.

Herod
I think—and the specter of the Galilean intervenes.
The nightmare is the head of John staring at me
      from the silver charger.
  "Half my kingdom," I said to Salome
      for giving pleasure to my guests.
All she wanted was his head.
All she wanted was the head.

Jesus
My line traces back through many generations
    to Solomon and David to give Me kingly stature.
And when the family tree branches
      to Jacob and Rebekah,
My right-to-be hangs upon a lie.

Herod
That unnecessary end to John haunted me.
I dreamed about that night a hundred times.

Then one day I heard of the Nazarene;
    Jesus they called Him, and the Christ.
The word was: "He's John's cousin" and,
    "How closely He resembles the Baptizer."
    "He preaches much like John," they said—
        "repentance and the kingdom of the living God."
    Fearless, they said He was, and that He called
      people to account for their misdeeds.
Then, in the long reaches of a night, it came to me.
Has John the Baptist come back, quickened from the dead,
    to haunt me?
Is this man, who died quite needlessly, alive again
    by some strange miracle of God?
I have to see Him, I thought . . . this Jesus,
      who preaches so like John,
    and even seems, as some have said,
      to look like him.

Jesus
The Herodian line was,
    by the strange way My Father willed it,
      Idumean.
If Herod were to trace his genealogy
      through the changing generations,
    he would come at last to Edom,

and in a twist of irony, arranged by God, to Esau.

Herod
Came Passover time, in that well-remembered year.
I was in Jerusalem, to seek favor with my people.
I asked Pilate to occupy my palace in the Holy City
    (a political ruse to gain his notice),
        while I occupied some lesser quarters down the street.
Herodias and I were wakened by the dawn
    and sat at breakfast in our temporary house.
There came a runner with the news
    that Pontius Pilate had a prisoner
    from my jurisdiction.
"Who is the man?" I asked,
    giving the question little force,
    nor yet expecting any special answer.
"Jesus, the Nazarene, who is called the Christ!"
    the herald said.

My God! It was the Nazarene.

Jesus
By what strange process does a lie come to an end?
What does a man say to another who, by the lie,
    is at best a puppet king
        and rules a puppet state,
    and who by a willful act of an ancient progenitor
        lost claim to being a member
           of God's chosen nation?

Herod
There He was. A ringer for the Baptist.
His shoulders drooped—and yet they didn't droop.
His eyes were tired, yet they looked at mine intensely.
But the face, the manner, the attitude . . .
    was quite unquestionably John's.
It gave me a start; my heart pounded,
    and only with great effort
    did I control my trembling hands.
John the Baptist resurrected? Is it possible?
I questioned Him. A hundred questions.
Are You John the Baptist?
Who is Your father, and who Your mother, Man?
Did You languish in the prison at Macchaerus?
Do You remember the night Salome danced?
Do You have no answer for Your king?

The word is that You work miracles, Man.
    Do me a miracle.
    Any miracle.
    I demand a sign.
    Wither that plant;
        make rain fall;
        levitate this maiden:
        something,
        anything.
            Prove to me
            that You are not
            the Baptist . . .
            or that You are.

Jesus
How do I, who am the Christ by virtue of My birthright,
    answer to such demands from a superstitious king?
Dare I do a miracle to prove My Deity, My Sonship,
    in obedience to this king?

Herod
I demand a miracle, a sign.

Jesus
Jacob, long before, bound Me to silence in that moment.

Herod
One sign.

Jesus
I must keep silence. . . .

Herod
Destroy the temple and build it again.

Jesus
These were My alternatives:
    A sign for Herod, and he would have quailed before it,
        setting Me free for sheer terror at it.
    A sign for My accusers, and their case
        would indeed have been lost.
    A sign from Me, and My obedience to the Father,
        which was to take Me to the cross
        for the transgressions of the world,
            would have been forfeit.
    And all, all would have been lost.
    No sign! No word! I held My peace!

Herod
A sign. A sign. A sign.

Silence, priests. Stop your accusations.
    I think perhaps you protest
        beyond the point of truth.

One sign.

Jesus
In that silence I sealed My doom.
Herod was My last great hope for freedom,
    but had I listened to him
    and changed one tumbler full of water into wine,
    or caused one plant to wither beside the atrium,
    his chance for salvation,
        and that of all the world,
            would have died, quite like the plant,
           a kind of turning bread to stone.
I held My peace; from this moment on
    the cross became inevitable;
    and if the cross is good obedience to My Father's will,
    then I am victor in the strife.

Herod
What a fool I was. What a fool!
No miracle.
No sign.
No answer to a single question posed.
Therefore no threat to me.
John the Baptist is dead, and I am free.
Had I made a spectacle of myself?
I did not know, nor did I care.
I was free.

All thanks to Pontius Pilate, who sent the fool to me.
A joke. A joke. A robe to hang about His shoulders.
Make Him out a King. . . .
Hang one of my old cloaks on Him.
It's not too early in the morning for Pontius
    to catch a politician's humor.
Oh, that's beautiful!
Here, fetch a golden chain to hang about His neck.
Now take Him back to Pontius Pilate,
    and he will know I know of his dilemma
    and concur in his decision.

What is the life of one fool?
Good-bye Jesus, King Jesus.
On Your way, fool.

Jesus
Ah, Herod. You took John the Baptist seriously.
You sent him to the dungeon;
    you bound his feet and hands in chains.
You sentenced him to death by the headsman's sword.
Me you did not take seriously.
    You mocked Me.
    You belittled Me.
When I left your presence, My martyrdom was sealed.
The Prophet would die within the city,
    no, by the city, but outside its walls.
I do not remember seeing you at Golgotha.
    But Herod, son of Esau, I prayed for you,
        that My Father would spare your life
        and give you a chance to repent.
On the cross I felt the full blows
    of His righteous judgment
        against your sins.
Why didn't you stop to ask questions of yourself?
You might thereby have learned the answers to the questions
    you addressed to Me.
I went forth to Calvary . . .
    there to bear your sins,
    and those of all My ancestors,
    that you and they in My death
        might find reconciliation . . .
    yea, that all men might find peace with God
        and good accord with every brother.

Herod
How bitter is the gall that fills my cup.
I think; I think; I think.
"Think ahead," Herodias bids me.
I dare not think ahead, for there lies death.
"Think back," this churning mind of mine demands.
"Back," say I, "to failure—or to victory?"
No, the only victory I won that day—
    and how hollow that turned out to be!—
    was that Pontius Pilate called me friend.

                            Amen.

4

Pilate and the King

An Introduction
Pontius Pilate was on the scene of history about ten years (A.D. 26-36), all of that time in Palestine, an emissary of Rome to the Jews. Many other such officials came and went, but Pilate, because of his encounter with Jesus, is known wherever people read Scripture or recite the Creed.

His origins and end are unknown. One story says he was the illegitimate son of Tyre, King of Mayence, who, after some adventures in Rome, was given the difficult task of governing troublesome Palestine. He apparently did a tolerable job, but several indiscretions, such as hanging a list of the Roman gods in the temple and slaying several men while offering sacrifices, brought his position to a precarious pass. His treatment of Jesus seems indeed to have been conditioned by his shaky relations with the Jews.

After the trial, Pilate stayed on in Palestine another six years. He was recalled to Rome and, except for legendary accounts of his death, is heard from no more. Legend says he was banished from Rome, fled to Lucerne, Switzerland, and lived in solitude on the mountain that bears his name. After some years of despair and depression he leaped from a precipice into the lake.

In our contrapuntal dialogs we have, using the literary devices available to us, imagined the people of the passion musing about the moment in their lives in which they came into contact with Jesus. The counterpoint is added by the parelleling thoughts of Jesus. Thus Pilate, in a modest villa on Mount Pilatus overlooking the clear blue waters of the lake, might have had thoughts like these.

Pilate is speaking.

The Dialog

Pilate
Water!
How many times must I tell that lazy lad
    to keep that basin filled with water
    and to place a towel beside it.
Must a man always wash in places
    specially suited to that end?
Is it so queer that I rinse my soiled hands
    here on the porch?

The water of the lake calls me!
    I host a silent fear that one day
        before the leaves turn color yet again
    I will answer its beckoning voice
        and hurl myself into it.

This very morning Claudia reminded me
    of our Palestinian duty tour for Rome.
She had had another dream in which I was involved,
    and she sought to warn me against some vile act
    I might perpetrate against myself.
That first dream was in Jerusalem during the trial
        of the Galilean Prophet.
    Then she saw me ending my political career
    unless I disentangled myself from the spider's web
    woven by that scheming Caiaphas
    to murder the Prophet of Galilee.

Water, lad!

Jesus
It was essential to the divine plan that I die
    in Jerusalem,
        at the hand of the world power.
To have died at the hands of the high priest
    would have been to die behind his cloistered walls,
    and the worldwide significance of My atonement
    could too easily have been lost.
So it was that Pontius Pilate was drawn into the trial,
    and in the end became the high priest
    who officiated at the sacrifice,
        though he was a quite reluctant priest.
Again the question of predestination is begged,
    and once again the problem of foreknowing
    in the mind and hand of God
        becomes an issue.
Do not read the account from that point of view;
    to do so will blind you to the facts that make
    the offering at Calvary vicarious for your sins.

Pilate
That was the day I sold my soul;
    and Claudia tried to warn me.
By the time her message reached me
    I was committed to my course.

Is it a basic truth that every magistrate
        is tempted by the fates to weigh the balances
        in favor of his own career?
They brought the Man to me,
        those scheming leaders of the people.
They charged Him with subverting the people of the nation,
        refusing to give tribute to our noble Caesar,
        and saying that He Himself held office as a king!
The whole thing was an obvious frame-up.
        That tender-eyed Prisoner a threat to Rome?
        Preposterous!
His accusers' eyes betrayed them;
        some nefarious scheme was obviously under way.
But the game was politics;
        the winning move, as I saw it,
        was to placate and win.
But, as I should have known—
        experienced politician that I was—
        when others make the opening move
        and play by a different system,
                the countermoves are often ineffective.
The rules by which they played were not mine,
        and I felt that I must play a little scheming of my own
        to beat them at this game
        in which they played for keeps.

Jesus
While Caiaphas and company babbled on about the charges,
        I took account of what had happened
        since the rooster crowed to greet the dawn.
Only a short time before I had stood before the Sanhedrin
        and watched Caiaphas draw himself to highest stature
        and listened as he cried in mocking anguish
        that I had blasphemed God,
        that My own testimony had convicted Me
        of a sin against the First Table of the Law
        and the First Commandment written on it.
"I demand to know—under oath—if You are the Christ,
        the Son of the living God," he fairly shouted.
In the court of the holy church,
        in the sacred precincts of the holy council,
        I was labeled as One who had blasphemed the very
                majesty of God.

By the time I had been brought before Pilate,

emissary of Rome,
the charges had shifted to the Second Table
of the holy Law,
and I was labeled One who blasphemed kings,
the Fourth Commandment altogether flouted by My action.

Pilate
The case demanded attention; it was most easily disposed of
then and there.
Two charges were filed against the Man:
One . . . He subverted the people.
Two . . . He stood in the way of the collection
of taxes for Caesar.
(Rather good moves to open the game.)
I remembered the case of Judas the Galilean,
son of Ezechias,
who not too long ago
had become the leader of a rebellion against Rome,
and harangued the people to refuse Rome's taxes.
Mighty ripples of his subversion
still disturbed the people.
It was highly conceivable that this Jesus of Galilee
could have espoused that cause,
and the old rebellion have exploded
at any moment.
I decided to get down to cases immediately.
"Are You the King of the Jews?" I asked Him.

Jesus
"King as *you* use the word or as the *Jews* use it?"

Pilate
"Am I a Jew?"

But I was studying the board. This Man knew how
to play the game too.
He had posed the question and reduced the answer.
I had to seek the truth on His terms now.
King—as a threat to Rome—
or King—as King of the Jews . . .
or was there still another possibility?

"Your own people and their chief priests brought You here.
Why? What have You done?"

Jesus
"I am not an earthly king.
If I were, My followers would have fought
    when I was apprehended in the garden.
But My kingdom is not of the world."

Pilate
I knew it. I knew it. The third possibility!
Neither King of the Jews nor threat to Rome.
Dreamer, maybe. Visionary. But no threat! No case!

"But You are a king, then?"

Jesus
"Yes, I was born for that purpose.
I came to bring truth to the world.
My followers are lovers of the truth."

Pilate
"What is truth?"

Jesus
Pilate, what have you done?
What is truth? you asked,
    and did not wait for My answer.

Only a few hours ago the high priest
    had demanded truth of Me,
        and when he heard it, he labeled Me blasphemer.
"I demand," he had said, "under oath and panalty,
    and before the God who judges truth and lies,
    that You tell us if You are the Christ,
        the Son of God."
When I gave him answer, he set his course
    to accomplish My death by a set of lies
    delivered under oath to Pilate.

Pilate
You speak of truth? What is truth?

Jesus
How alike My judges; how limited the mind of man!
Caiaphas and Pilate, different in a hundred ways,
    were but the same in matters such as these.
One from the East, one from the West.
One in Roman toga, the other in the robe of priest.

the other lived with sword and golden rings.
Caiaphas writhed in convolutions until he found
    rest in the most expedient plan
    by which to condemn Me.
Pilate began his examination quite unruffled,
    but at his own question began his own contortions
    that brought about My death.
Neither gave Me credence, nor did they accept
    the all-consuming verity
    that I am the Way, the Truth, the Life.
Neither of them accepted My Messiah-hood, My Kingship,
    but saw Me as a person of the plains
        rather than the heights,
    an ordinary, meaningless man,
    to be offered to appease their separate ends.
So they passed Me by on the other side
    and I was left to die of wounds
    far deeper than the flesh.

Pilate

I have dealt with thousands of men
    and thousands of judicial cases.
In two questions and two answers
    I was convinced that the Man
        was not quilty as charged.
With an eye to getting back to my work,
        and on with the day,
    I went back to the porch
        where Caiaphas and friends
           waited for my verdict.
I made it as plain as I knew how.
"He is not guilty of any crime."
But I wasn't prepared for the screaming
    and the babble that ensued.
This early in the morning, a crowd gathered already!
    And the crowd wanted blood!

Jesus

Two questions, two answers;
    My credentials were established.
    My case was acquitted. I was free.
    Pilate had come to My rescue.
Then I heard the screams of the people on the porch
    where Pilate announced his findings.
    And I knew this was not the end.

Judgment against the sins of the world
    was not this easily satisfied.
The cup had only been tasted and found bitter;
    it was still there to drink.

Fortify Me, Father, against the gall in this chalice,
    and hold Me steady to the drinking.

Pilate
Water! Water! Must I carry water for myself?
The lad had better bend to the task,
    or I will see he does not bend again.

I heard it out of the corner of the crowd . . . and I hoped
       for a moment
    it would save my day and help me in that hour
    to keep face with myself and with those animals
       that screamed for blood.
It turned out the Man was from Galilee.
This was Herod's house, loaned to me for these days
       of celebration and unrest.
And Herod was tetrarch of Galilee.
    This Galilean was still protected by the law,
    and the law provided that a man had right to trial
    in his own province.
I sent Him forthwith to Herod,
    with a suitable note saying it semed to me
    he might do me a favor by handling
    the case of this Man Jesus
       since He was from his jurisdiction.

Jesus
The law is said to be benevolent.
Like a warm blanket, it protects the innocent
    and in comparable coldness
    metes out justice to the evil,
The law is meant to be
    man's friend, an umbrella to shield him
       from the beating sun and driving rain, or
    man's enemy,
       if by his actions he opens himself
          to its exact demands.
By Caiaphas' clever manipulation I was summarily exiled
    from the laws of the spiritual community,
    and by his careful stratagem I was exposed

to the laws that govern all humanity.
Pilate found Me innocent of any crime
    for which by the law I might be restrained or executed,
    yet on a technicality, he sought to save his skin
        at My expense.
There was no interest in the law,
        in the right and dignity of My person,
    in the court of Herod,
    and I became a plaything of these men,
    for Herod, with his robes and laughter, tore My soul
    and let Me know that the law could be ignored
        if expediency demanded it.

Pilate
Herod turned out to be a wit,
    what with the Prisoner returned to me
        decked in one of his old robes.
    And I remember making note to have Herod in to dinner
        at my earliest convenience.

But the King of the Jews was mine again.
Thinking to have the matter done, I determined to play
    upon the people's love for underdogs.
"Flog Him," I ordered.
They took Him to the back courtyard. I expected to hear
        Him scream,
    and to call Him forth when the moaning started.
There was no noise from the back, no crying
        for mercy or relif.
When far more than enough time
        for a simple flogging had gone by,
    I ordered Him brought out
        to stand before the gathered crowd.
The soldiers had amused themselves, waiting for my orders,
    by twisting together, into a kind of crown,
        strands of bramble,
    and jamming it upon His head . . .
    and by hanging Herod's cloak about His shoulders
    had added grisly humor to that joke.
They had overstepped my orders, but that was of little note,
    for He was a most unkingly sight
    and thus suited my purposes the better.
I took Him before the people at the porch,
    sent Him to the balustrade,
    paused a dramatic pause,

made a gesture to include His crowned head,
   His bleeding body and bowed back,
      His thong-bound hands and bared feet . . .
"Behold the Man," I said.

Jesus
As the high priest had placed Me outside the canon laws,
   as Herod, by not calling in the law, had excluded Me from it,
   so the Roman governor placed Me outside the secular law,
      declared Me a *persona non grata,*
      an out-law to the law,
         in the fateful order to have Me flogged.
He found in Me no fault.
He did not rescind his declaration.
He placed Me outside the reach of all law.
   Through the official legate of the Roman Empire,
      the law spoke to Me . . .
      I do not know You, from whence You come;
      I never knew You, depart, and be accursed.
Over and over the law screamed at Me, "You do not exist,"
   as the lash descended on My back.
The crown of thorns and the voices of mocking soldiers
   screamed at Me, "You are a nothing."
The people whom I willed to love
   denied Me at the balustrade
   and, in their cry for My death,
   expelled Me from the laws of love and mercy.

Hold Me steady, Father, for I have taken another swallow
   of the bitter stuff that fills the cup;
      I grow frightened at the power of it,
      but I must drink it for the world's salvation.

Pilate
In the midst of pressure I comfortably held my own,
   at least when I was younger.
There was still a ruse by which I might extricate myself
   from this all-consuming web.
Barabbas, archenemy of every man's security,
   murderer, insurrectionist, a threat to peace,
   was available for bartering.

Water, slave, water. Do you hear me?

The custom of releasing a prisoner at the Passover
　　was about to be observed,
　　and I would be free of this Man.

Jesus
The Passover of My people was hard upon us.
Since the days of Moses when the first exodus occurred,
　　and at the bidding of My Father,
　　My people took a lamb without spot or blemish
　　　　for Passover use.
Its blood was drawn and smeared
　　upon the lintels of their doors,
　　and the angel of death passed over the house
　　whereon the blood was smeared.
Little did they know, that crowd of people on the pavement,
　　that they were making choice for sacrifice,
　　for all their sins.
Barabbas or Me.
The proper sacrificial Lamb was chosen when they called
　　for My crucifixion
　　and the release of Barabbas,
　　　　blemished by his gross misdeeds.
Yet once again the cup is at My lips,
　　and once again I drink,
　　to save all people from their sins.
O Father, hold My hand.

Pilate
I wanted done with the whole miserable thing.
I signaled for water and towel to be brought,
　　and with the ancient sign
　　that absolved of any guilt in murder,
　　I washed my hands before them all.
They took the Galilean, half dead already, I should think,
　　from my presence, led Him down the street
　　to crucifixion hill; I think they called it Golgotha.
Word came before lunch that He was hanging on the cross,
　　and that the centurion in charge
　　　　had included the two robbers
　　condemned to die by order of the state.
At the tenth hour men came begging for the body
　　　　of the Nazarene.

It was incredible that He should be already dead,
    but if that were the case,
    the body they could have.

Must I fetch water for myself?

                                            Amen.

5

Satan and God's Protagonist

An Introduction

Satan is no imaginary creature. No one has seen him, yet who does not know his nefarious devices to destroy good? He moves onto the pages of Scripture and history before the first one is turned. When his story comes at last to its end and the book is about to be closed, he will still be there.

His origins are shrouded in mystery. Doctrinally we say he was created (which makes him creature, by no means on a level with God) during the creation week, that he fell away from God, has since been intent on destroying the works of God, notably those who come in faith to Jesus Christ. His end will be in "the bottomless pit" or "eternal torment in hell." His name is also "Legion" for there are many devils, for whom Satan seems to exercise leadership.

If Satan was active in the fall of man from grace, it is certainly to be expected to find him active at the restoration to grace, that is, in Christ's time and at His passion. He slipped into the wilderness, where Christ wrestled with the question of His Sonship, with the same ease with which he slipped into Eden. The unswerving dedication of Jesus to the Son/Servant revelation only frustrated him, and he would not rest until Jesus was dead.

You cannot compare the temptations of the devil and the trials of God, unless you do it for contrast. In his temptations, Satan not only tries to conceal what is the main issue of contention, but tries to give a false impression of the situation. Illusion is presented as reality. He consistently seeks to conceal the main objective of God's justice. God does not deal in false impressions, although His ends may be temporarily concealed. God's trials are done to induce people to redirect their feet to the main highway, on which they are led to God's ultimate goal for the human race. Jesus understood the difference; His victory lies in His rejecting the one and accepting the other.

The dialog does not take place in far-off realms amid angels or devils, or before the great Throne, whereon the Father sits. It happens on the earth among people, for there is where Jesus, Son of God, is, and you can be sure it is also where Satan is. This very building, this very room, notwithstanding that it is the church, might house the dialog.

Satan is speaking.

The Dialog

Satan

By the most judicious use of friendly persuasion
　　I have succeeded in causing a group of those
　　who worship me to establish a congregation,
　　known as the First Church of Satan.
The congregation is not large,
　　but it is a foothold on the minds and souls of men,
　　which gives me status with my fellows
　　　　and proves the point I have been making,
　　that God is not by any means
　　the only or the final answer.
I have, furthermore, enlisted at least ten million Americans
　　who gather in groups of three or four,
　　with me in the midst of them,
　　to dabble in occult arts . . .
　　　　they use ouija boards for answers
　　　　　　to their questions about life;
　　　　they dabble in the ancient art of witchcraft,
　　　　　　so that the witch of Endor lives again;
　　　　they hold Black Masses,
　　　　　　with me enthroned upon the altar;
　　　　they drink blood from silver chalices,
　　　　　　in a communion service done to honor me
　　　　　　and strengthen their faith in my power.
Who said my day was done?
Who claims the devil is dead?

Jesus

All creatures left the Father's hand as things of beauty.
Every tree, every animal, every fish and bird, was perfect
　　as it swam or walked or grew or flew upon the earth.
Of consummate beauty were God's holy angels,
　　strong, gleaming, intelligent,
　　wondrous indeed to behold.
When the mighty chorus of cherubim and seraphim,
　　and splendid angels round the Throne,
　　struck the first chord of heavenly music
　　to praise the majesty of their majestic King,
　　no more spectacular sound has ever been heard.
Their sounds rivaled but transcended the songs
　　of the morning stars singing together.
The majesty and mystery of their music
　　reached into the distant corners of glory

and continued through the ages,
to be overshadowed only by the new song in My honor,
done to greet Me on My return
to heaven from the planet earth.
Nowhere in all the reaches of heaven
was there one discordant note.
To grace the earth's creation My Father formed a man
and gave to him his helpmeet
to be mother of all mankind.
Their laughter echoed through the garden
where He placed them,
as their life and love reflected well
the image of their God.
In all the universe from morning stars to man and woman,
nothing marred the splendor
of the Father's great creation.

Satan

I have adjusted to the life I have to live.
I call it the exciting and the good life.
Unlike people, I do not have to sift and weigh
between good and evil.
Once I was committed to my course,
I decided to make the most of it,
and it has been glorious.
I am free of the terrors of hell; I am prince of it!
I have no terror over death, for I am spirit and cannot die.
I have no concern for eternity; it is decided for me,
and I cross no bridges until I place my feet upon them.
And in the meanwhile, with great abandon, I work at my
avowed purpose,
making headway when and where I can to build my kingdom.

Jesus

In the midst of the soaring choruses of the hosts of angels
there came one day a most distressing discord—
for Satan, with a host of celestial beings,
defied the Father, and must by divine decree
be driven from the light.
Life was not denied him, but the privileges of heaven were,
and he was left to wander to and fro upon the earth.
That he should tempt Our man and woman was inevitable,
for prohibition at the tree of life
had been set as limits to the garden
and to God,

and Satan knew it.
We watched him move about the garden many times,
       plotting course.
We could not interfere,
       for that would have made human beings
              mere automatons.

Satan
My first victory was in Eden.
It seemed to me,
       that if I wanted place and power
       in the scheme of things,
       those creatures in the garden
       might also yearn for even better things
       if better things were dangled
       close enough for them to see.
Man and woman were no match for me.
       A question or two to break down their defenses,
       a thought or two to raise their hopes,
       and I had two converts.

Jesus
Come Satan did, and the human pair,
       forgetting in ignorance,
       by some devious process of the mind,
       betrayed the trust My Father placed in them.
They disobeyed My Father,
              and in righteous indignation,
              and in the scales of perfect justice,
       must pay the price for their unfortunate actions.
Mankind must die.

The dilemma posed for My Father was intense. He is just
       to perfection;
       but He held then, as He does now,.
       an immense love for His man-creatures.
Justice demanded death; so He had spoken.
Love strained after the human creatures,
       for it had been the Father's purpose
       that they should share the glory of Our heaven.
Justice cries for justice and must be heard.
Not to satisfy justice is to deny it.
But love cries too, and must be heard,
       and the price upon it may be indeed
       as demanding as death.

This was the dilemma: How can justice be satisfied,
        and love be satisfied,
    when both are perfect and complete?

Satan
The victory was mine. Adam and Eve belonged to me.
I knew God. He would have an irresolvable problem
    on His hands.
I am walking proof of His justice. . . .
But His love?
That's something I'll never understand.
        He might have, I am certain, doomed the human race
            to everlasting anguish,
                had not His mercy intervened.

But I am finite, and cannot know the mind of God.
When in righteous anger He chastised His creatures,
    He had already resolved the dilemma
            I had imposed upon Him,
        for He promised the human race escape
            from the wrath to come,
        and for the first time
            I discovered God's ultimate plan for me.

Jesus
The dilemma was resolved in the following manner.
If One would place Himself
            under the divine demands of justice
        and substitute for those who thus deserved to die;
        if One could, impelled by My Father's love,
        go and satisfy the perfect law,
        then man and woman could go free and the plan
        to add their voices to the angel choruses
        and to set them free in glory
            could be attained.
It would have to be accomplished by a love so great
        that it would bear the wound of death,
            and the fury of the prince of hell and darkness.
There was no other way.

"Will You go?" My Father asked.
"I will go!" I said.

Satan
I am not privy to the plans of heaven, save as God
    chooses to reveal them.

It is not in any way possible to infiltrate God's domain.
When I have been there, it has always been openly,
for I cannot disguise myself before God
to be a holy angel.
I waited many centuries for the resolution of the Plan,
busy all the time about the business
to which I am totally committed.
My activities were singularly successful;
read between the lines and know that I speak truth.
But God revealed His plan's progression
when the holy angels sang of peace on earth.
I knew then I was on the verge
of my greatest adventure.

Jesus
My incarnation was an invasion of territory
in which Satan ran rampant and unfettered.
He had claimed it at the Fall,
and now by a kind of eminent domain
thought he held title to it.

I had received My credentials
at My baptism
with the affirmation that I was
God's well-beloved Son,
spoken in My Father's voice out from the clouds.
I had to wrestle with the problem of My Sonship!
In what does Sonship consist;
what rights and privileges were Mine;
what responsibilities belonged to Me as Son?
Sons had special privileges.
They lived in their father's domain,
with privilege to come and go;
with rights to come for comfort and for peace
to the father's breast,
to come by prayer to speak together of devotion.
Sons had responsibilities,
for fathers claim the right to obedience
from their sons,
and I must be obedient, steadfast, certain, sure
in every act, in every word, in every thought.
With humble gratitude I, Jesus, Child of Mary, Man,
claimed the privilege for My own,
and accepted the responsibility.

For days and days I wrestled
    with the question in the wilderness.
The privilege of My Father's heart was Mine.
In the deep retreat of prayer I stood at last convinced.
My encounter with Satan in the wilderness
    buttressed My conviction.

Satan

Trial and error. Trial and error.
Every man has his weak spot.
How did the ancient prophecy go?
    "Thou shalt bruise His heel!"
Where was the weak spot in The Man? Where best to cause
    a faltering step?
One faltering step, and He was mine!
One trembling word, and no one would believe Him.
I must find the way to bring failure to the Plan.

I saw Him in the barren reaches of the wilderness.
Try for victory . . .
    If You are the Son of God, turn these stones to bread,
        and eat.
It didn't work.
    If You are the Son of God, check out the angels;
        surely they will offer You protection.
It didn't work.
    If You want lordship of the earth, I can give You
        a shortcut; bow before me.
It didn't work.
I left the area, determined to try again.

Jesus

When Satan had gone, angels came and cared for Me.
    Satan came tempting Me to failure,
        but I was faithful to My trust.
    The Father had tested Me, and I was certain now
        of My responsibility.
My baptism had been to death;
    the wilderness experience confirmed the direction
        to which I had been committed.
Nor had I seen the last of My antagonist.

Satan

Make Him stumble . . . just once . . . and He would be defeated.
But how?
I decided since my failure in the wilderness

to try guerilla warfare.
I would attack Him from various and unsuspected sources.
    I took possession of a little lad, fourteen or so.
    I irritated him so badly he thrashed and drooled,
        and threw himself upon the ground.
    I did not kill him, only tormented him
        almost to the breaking point.
Then I engineered an encounter with the Christ,
    only to be embarrassed by His power to drive me out
    and free the lad.
Strike again . . .
    through a little maiden—
    and embarrassment and anger at her return to life.
Strike again . . .
    with Legion at my side
    and a calculated attempt to hold possession of a man.
    (I blush to remember the incident.)
    He bade us enter into pigs, and we were forced to go.
    We drove the frightened animals into a nearby lake
        in our righteous indignation.
Strike again, and again I did . . .
    but His compassion for the peace of every man
        was boundless,
    and the power and patience I had hoped to try
            beyond endurance,
        thus to make Him stumble on His course,
            was like a mighty river flowing.

Jesus
The days of My ministry were long and full;
    I saw sin and sickness everywhere.
The lame and halt, the deaf and blind,
    the crippled arms and tortured legs,
    the whole gamut of diseases, even death,
    were all about and cried for loving care.
I touched an ailing woman to make her well,
    and power went out from Me to do it.
I bade a bedfast man arise and walk,
    and paid the price in power.
Lepers came crying out their loathsome malady,
    and I had compassion for them;
    and as I healed them, I perceived again
        that power had gone out of Me.
And again and again the fallen angel Satan

came himself or sent his hosts
to attack Me through some most unfortunate person
he had seized to torment—thus to torment Me . . .
pushing Me to the breaking point.
Were it not that I remembered I was Son
to the heavenly Father,
with privilege of prayer and deep devotion,
and had I not gone to be alone with Him
in long night watches given to prayer,
asking and receiving,
I might have gone beyond the point of breaking
and lost the cause entrusted to My care.
But having gone in prayer for power from its Source,
I found new strength for each new day,
with the great demands upon Me in it,
and power to bid dark Satan know and keep his place.

Satan
Trial and error. . . . Persist!
Try another approach. His disciples seemed a likely place
from which to swoop at Him
and bring the stumbling step about.
At Caesarea Philippi, with more subtlety than was my wont,
I entered into Simon Peter, and through him
suggested that He really didn't have to die. . . .
"Not You, Jesus, Son of the living God, not You."
He looked at Peter,
and spoke those words I had heard from Him
so oft before,
"Satan, behind Me."

If the attack did not work through one,
then perhaps another.
I studied the disciples—
Andrew, Philip, Bartholomew—Judas . . .
Judas! There was my man.
I slipped into Judas, and with calculated care
helped him to reason that he could fill the coffers
of the treasury he maintained for the disciples
by selling Jesus.
After all, hadn't your Lord and Master slipped
away from crowds that wanted to kill Him
before . . .
remember the Nazareth time when they wanted

to throw Him over the cliffs?
He hasn't really lived up to your expectations,
    has He, Judas?
What has He really done to free your people
    from the Romans?
I won. Judas made arrangements to identify his Master
    to the High Priest.
Caiaphas and scheming Annas were no problem.
    They were on my side,
    and I didn't speak a word to them.
Pilate took a little doing, but not much.
    A suggestion that it was politically expedient for him
    to let this one slip through,
        and the hour was mine.
Herod might at least have given me a moment's pause,
    but he never swerved from his evil intentions.
The field, the day, the victory, if you please,
    were mine.

Jesus
I left My place in the mystery of the Holy Trinity,
    and was incarnate of the Holy Spirit in the Virgin Mary,
    that I might redeem mankind from the righteous judgment
        of My righteous Father.
To accomplish this, I must place Myself under the judgment
    meted out to humanity through the first man—
    that he, and all, must, for sins done,
        be banished beyond the Father's love
    and spend eternity in hell, where rules the
        Prince of Darkness.
From judgment and from hell, once committed,
    there was no return.
Mankind might be rescued from it, before it became reality,
    if One could go for all, through death and hell,
    and thus appease the judging wrath
        of My beloved Father.
For that cause and to that end, I had volunteered Myself.

The great timetable-keeping clock
    by which My Father kept His plan
    had struck the hour of judgment
        against the sins of man.
I went into the garden called Gethsemane to pray,
    fearful of the hour.

Three times
     I called upon My Father, in prayer most fervent.
Three times
     I sought to open communication with Him.
Three times
     I stormed the gates of heaven. . . .
"I am Your Son," I cried, "I am Your only Son,
     Your beloved Son. . . .
Must I drink the cup?
Is there no other way?
Do You hear Me, Father, as I pray?
Where are You, Father?
As never in My incarnation,
     I need You now, I need You near!
Father?
Father!
I will drink the cup to final dregs,
     but spare Me Your silence, Father of Mine.
Why are You silent, when I need You most?
Whether You hear Me or not, Father, let Me say it.
     If I must, I will drink the cup.
     Your will must be done."
That My Father heard, I knew. For even as I prayed
     an angel came and in silence
     pointed to the city and My death.
I knew My course. My life was forfeit for mankind.

Satan
The angel in the garden where He prayed was clue.
God was not listening, and the way was clear for me.
With the yawning maw of hell quite visible behind me,
     I walked to meet Him at the cross.
Exactly at the noon hour, the sun was eclipsed by a cloud,
     and darkness covered the entire area . . .
     and at high noon I moved in. . . .
God did not say me nay.
He was mine . . . the Son of God was mine.
An hour sped by and then a second and a third.
All the while I screamed at Him,
     "Where is Your Father now,
          Son of God?
     Curse God and live!"
I laughed at Him,
     as I conjured pictures of the damned for Him—

hosts and legions in hell's reaches—
and every one a mockery of the divine plan
and of holy, misplaced love.
Where is Your God, Jesus?
Curse Him and die!

Jesus
Eli, Eli, lama sabachthani.

Satan
God abandoned His Son to me, do you hear?

Jesus
Eli, Eli.

Satan
Jesus was mine . . . in hell . . . abandoned by all humanity,
abandoned by God . . . and left to me.

(Pause)

Well, we got pretty dramatic, I should say,
but does anybody believe this kind of thing?
After all, this is the 20th century,
and talk about witches,
and soothsayers,
and devils and gods
is hardly a fit subject for this day and age.
A God who condemns people to the nether regions?
a God with a Son?
a God that kills?
a God that dies?
No friend, these are the good days,
with freedom all around to be yourself . . .
live it up, you are only another meaningless animal
in the evolutionary scale.
Have fun—any way you choose—you will not surely die.
You see, even I am illusion and a dream,
an imaginary figment, without form or substance;
when I stop talking, you won't really know
whether you heard a spirit or not.
A spirit? What is that?
No, good friend, life is yours to take; take it while you can.
There is no God—check all the laboratories of the world
and you will not find Him.
And when you come right down to it, friend,

you can double check and you won't find me
in any scientific search.
So get rid of your hang-ups, forget your conscience,
throw out the Law, unfrustrate yourself
and live it up.
I tell you straight: You are free.

(Pause)

Jesus
Everyone who commits sin is a slave to sin,
but if the Son makes you free,
you will be free indeed.
Then you will have true life,
and have it abundantly.

Amen.

6

The Father and Jesus

An Introduction

Doctrine says that God is holy, which means He is separated from all other creatures and things; He is sometimes called the "wholly other One." It says, furthermore, that He is a vast, majestic, fascinating mystery, totally impenetrable by any of His creatures. He is, says doctrine, a spirit, without body or physical substance. In many respects He is best left that way, thought of that way, and worshiped that way.

It is very difficult to talk about God without some kind of handles. Handles have been developed in the form of anthropomorphisms and anthropopathisms, that is, God is given human parts and ways and emotions, that we might better understand Him. Anthropomorphisms are stepping stones to grasping many of the truths about God.

The blessed Trinity stays a mystery, quite unfathomable. No one can understand the interrelation of the Persons, nor yet the uniqueness of the oneness. Ascribing human ways and emotions to God doesn't help to comprehend the Trinity, but it does allow some thinking about, some minutest measure of comprehension, some little peephole into God's nature.

We know from Scripture that the decision to rescue man from the plight into which he plunged at the Fall was made in the councils of the holy Trinity. At least anthropomorphically, it can be said that They discussed the problem at great length, then having evolved a plan, proceeded to carry it out. (When we meet God face to face, He will tell us that is not how it was at all.) We are not privy to the great prayer sessions the Father had with Jesus, except for the high priestly prayer. We can only guess what the great silences of the Father meant to Jesus during His lifetime, especially during the passion.

The words that follow were written and are spoken with fear and trembling. "Who has known the mind of the Lord, or who has been His counselor?" (Rom. 11:34). Remembering that we speak as fools, and that we speak as if, and only as if, these members of the Trinity were humans, we present the Gospel in this dialog between Gabriel and Jesus, who is also the Christ.

Gabriel speaks first.

The Dialog

Gabriel

I am Gabriel, who stand at the right hand of the Father,
    created by His omnipotent hand,
    and committed with my whole being to His service.
I have seen the mighty acts of God, and none has impressed
    me more than the tender loving care
    He has extended to His creature man.
It was a thrilling hour to see God bend to the earth,
    to scoop up dust and shape it,
    then to breathe the breath of life into that lifeless clay,
    to see man rise from the river bank,
    stretch himself to fullest height,
    then slowly kneel to thank the God he didn't know
        for life and being.

In the fearful hour of man's fall from grace,
        when Adam broke the covenant agreement
        established by my God to help him understand
        the free choice he had been given,
    it was I who raised my hand
        for quiet through the ranks of angels,
    for the serenity of the tender, loving, all-wise God
        was shaken to its deepest roots.

I was there when the soul of Abel was borne to heaven,
    the victim of his brother's anger.
For the second time I saw the righteous wrath of God.

When the covenant was sealed
    between Abraham of Ur and God,
    that a Savior would be sent,
    I knew the great fine plan for man's redemption
    now was moving to fulfillment.

It was I who sent the angel messenger to shepherds
    in their nighttime watches on the slopes of Bethlehem
        to announce the birth of hope and peace,
    and then the tiers of golden voices
    to praise the God in highest heaven
        for His unspeakable Gift to Adam's children.

We watched the Son of God in human form
    assume His grave responsibility of proclamation,
    that all might know God's loving care and tender mercies

and His demonstration of them in His life and living,
and we saw Him celebrate the ancient meal of Israel
in the company of His faithful friends.

Jesus
My Father lives and works His purposes
only when the world is ready for them.
The hour in His great God-mind had come,
and I journeyed to Jerusalem,
there to carry out My mission.
I needs must spend a little time with My beloved men;
so it was that I arranged
that we might eat the Passover
yet one more time together.
We gathered on a rooftop porch
above a house I commandeered.
There was time, that afternoon,
before the shadows lengthened,
to speak to them of many things. . . .
I was much aware of the all-engulfing thoughts
that lay behind the words I said to them.
I loved them all in complete transmission
of My Father's love.
I loved Simon (who this night would deny Me with an oath),
and Judas (who had completed
arrangements for My betrayal),
and all the rest (who would run away this night,
lest they be apprehended
and forfeit life with Me).
I loved them in their weaknesses
and their enormous needs.
It came to Me
(as thoughts of overwhelming compassion engulfed Me)
that these twelve were symbols
of the teeming throngs of all humanity.
The Father had placed them all into My hands
as His special gift to Me.
In these next hours,
through the trial, on the cross, in hell,
I could not hold them safe.
In the pressures of My love,
and in an overwhelming wave of great concern,
and quite oblivious to My friends,
I lifted up My eyes, and heart and hands,

to My beloved Father.
"You have given Me this gift of men, O Father Mine,"
    I prayed.
"Now I cannot guard and keep them,
    as I move beneath Thy judgment out to hell.
Hold them safe for Me.
Hold them safe till I return."
My Father heard, and all were safe
    in His divine protection.

Gabriel
When the Passover meal was over,
    I watched from the battlements
    as Jesus led the way over the brook Kidron
    to the garden Olivet.
I watched, and saw a shadow cross the Father's face.
The very light in heaven seemed to grow a little dimmer.
I signaled pianissimo to the angel chorus,
    for the Father's countenance
        bespoke His growing hurt.
Jesus moved alone to a place beside an aged olive tree,
        and prayed His anguished prayer.
    We heard the words in heaven.
    They were fraught with fear,
        and a certain mounting terror,
            yet they concluded in obedience.
I was the first among the angels to grasp and know
    that this most fervent prayer
        from deep inside the heart of Jesus,
        reaching deep inside the heart of God,
    must be answered with an awesome "No."
The praying in the garden stopped,
    and Jesus paused for answer.
All the eyes of saints and angels
    looked toward the loving Father
        and awaited His reply.
    Always They had spoken back and forth
        in prayer, the Father and the Son.
    Always, when the Son had called, the Father heard
        and answered Him.
Wearily, slowly, the Father God raised His heavy head
    and looked at me, and gave a sign
    to send an angel to the garden. . . .
Such was the burden of the answer to that prayer,

that God the loving Father could not *say* His "No,"
nor yet could He in justice tell Him "Yes,"
for in the answer to that prayer
hung the eternity of every person on the earth,
and in the answer to that prayer
the warrant for the death of God was written.
To ease the horrible tension
    causing every creature in the heavens
    to tremble where they stood,
    I sent an angel to Gethsemane
    to bring the word that He must drink the cup.
Thus by a creature, one of myriads along the golden streets,
    the Son was sent to Calvary.

Jesus
Through My whole public life there had been
    sufficient signals from My Father's actions
        that the purchase price for the souls of human beings
        would be far more than even I could understand.
At My baptism He called Me Son and Servant.
My baptism was a "baptism into death."
On the mountain of transfiguration I was conscious
    of His changing attitude. . . .
        Though He spoke, as at the Jordan's edge,
            He now spoke *of* Me, not *to* Me,
            and in the subtle change I shuddered,
            for it was like a dark cloud passing
                over Me.
I was not unprepared for the angel in Gethsemane.
It was inevitable that My Father would leave Me
    to the struggle.
It was the knowing with such finality that the time had come.
    Anything was possible for Me, with My Father's strength
        to hold Me
    and with His good love to shield Me.
The rift was real on Olivet . . .
    and the only way, the only way I could stand
        the fact of cross and death
    was to know that He had heard Me . . .
        that He was there . . .
            that He knew.
Whatever would become of Me, if He didn't hear,
    if He didn't care,
        if He left Me all alone . . .

Gabriel
The whole trial was a nightmare for us who lived in glory.
We could see the gross maneuvering of Satan—
        of evil and indifferent men.
The crowd's rabble noises sounded up to heaven.
The Father heard them, and I think
    He tried to shut them out
    by a sheer determination not to hear—
    but couldn't, and perhaps He wouldn't,
    for He must suffer too,
        to gain the souls and hearts of men.
We heard Caiaphas scream, "Blasphemy" at Him,
    and cringed at the horror of the thought.
We saw Herod turn from frightened questioner
    to a mocking animal.
We heard the gentle sound of dripping water in a basin
    as Pilate washed his hands.
We heard the thump of beam on stone, as they led Him
    down the Way of Sorrows and past the city gates.
The angels tried to sing a little louder, but songs of praise
    could not hide the clank of iron hitting iron,
    to hold His body to the cross,
    or even wood on wood, to hold this cross erect
        beneath the oriental sun.
And all the while the crude, lewd, mocking jokes
    they made about the very Son of God!
I bade the angels hush their song. This was more the hour
    for a mournful dirge . . .
    not for songs of praise . . .
    and better yet for quiet.
Then in the hush, His voice—

Jesus
Father, forgive them, for they know not what they do.

Gabriel
There, did you hear?
He called upon His Father,
    though the Father had not answered
    since the prayer to hold His loved ones safe.
The Father sat in silence, hearing,
    yet He did not answer,
    nor give evidence of having heard.
It was a mighty prayer for those who used Him spitefully,

and persecuted Him with cross and mocking voices.
"Father, forgive. . . . Father, hold back Your judgment
        against these men
    until at last I have redeemed them.
I know You cannot let such malignant evil go
    without Your judgment weighed against it. . . .
But wait, O Father Mine, until I have won for them
    forgiveness."
So He prayed.
And no lightning bolt to strike them dead,
        no opening earth to swallow them,
    stopped the awful business on the hill.
With His simple prayer, God's Son bespoke
        His great determination
    to carry out the holy plan . . .
    and announced to heaven that He would . . .
            to save the damned souls of Pilate,
            and the soldiers with the nails and hammer,
            and all those who stood by, mocking,
            and the two thieves appointed by the Romans
                to accompany Him in death,
            and of every sinful man and girl,
            and you, and you, and you . . .
            that He would go all the way to death.
Even now, thinking of that awful day,
    I want to say . . .

Hush! Hush!
The worst was yet to come.
The Father raised His head, and bade the angel servants
    stretch a cloud between the cross and us.
        Thick and dark, the cloud,
            shutting out the sun on earth,
        but shutting out the view we had of Calvary.
The Father could not bear to look.
        He sat upon the dais, stony still.
        And I could only guess what horrible thoughts
            went through His mind,
        if He was capable of thinking them at all.
I thought to signal to the saints and angels
            to be still, but they had seen the Father,
            and in all the whole of heaven
                there was not a sound.
        Not one angel wing stirred the air to break the silence.

Not a single sigh from any saint.
Not in all the history of heaven, or ever since,
      did such silence reign.
Only this day.
Only this hour.

This is the truth of it:
      the Father had abandoned His Son to hell,
      He had given Him over, a plaything for Satan,
      all the sins with judgment accrued upon them
            of all the world
      were loaded on Him.
      Here was damnation to the uttermost.
Yet not a sound escaped Him hanging on the cross.
We could hear the drops of blood
      fall to the earth
      (or was it perspiration, or a tear?) . . .

Then the shattering cry that pierced the cloud
      and echoed back from wall to wall of heaven . . .

Jesus
My God, My God, why hast Thou forsaken Me?

Gabriel
Were it possible, the hush in heaven deepened,
      and I think I saw, if this be possible,
      a tear upon the cheek of God.
This is the heart-tearing truth of what we saw that day:
      Nobody wanted Jesus. There was not a single one
            to love Him and to give Him strength.
      His cherished church, His holy nation,
            and all humanity denounced Him,
                  degraded Him,
                  abandoned Him.
      His own close friends and pupils
            denied, betrayed, and fled
                  and left Him quite alone.
Now God the Father abandoned this, His Son . . .
      the holy right hand was not there in the darkness,
      the everlasting arms were not beneath Him,
      the great wings and the Father's love
            were not there to shield and warm Him.
The Father sat immobile on the throne,
      the Judge, and if you will, the Executioner,

reliving in a God-dimension
the sacrifice by Abraham of his son Isaac . . .
  except there was no ram
    among the rocks of Calvary.
The Father offered open rein to Satan
  against the very soul of Jesus,
  and Satan grasped the opportunity thus offered
  to magnify the terrors of all hell
    upon His holy being.

We waited, for who had words to speak to a Father
  who could love like that?
Not an angel stirred.
Not a saint moved.

And then His voice again . . .

Jesus
It is finished!

Gabriel
Was it a signal the Godhead had arranged,
  to signal consummation of the mighty act
  by which redemption was made possible for humans?
It was, whatever else, the shout of victory
  over sin and Satan, death and hell.
It was the announcement to the Father of a battle won,
  of the mightiest of missions brought to end.
And if anyone had dared to look, they might have seen
  a tear of joy well up and tumble down
  the Father's face.

The silence was ended, and angels went
  to lift the corner of the cloud
  and allow a ray of light to gleam on the horizon.
This was the mighty truth for every human being,
  that Satan would not lurk
  behind the door of death, for in the Christ
  his power had been shorn
  and death became man's friend.
Such is the love of Jesus, Son of God,
  that He went into death,
  to show that it is but a door
  through which all might pass
  in perfect peace and calm.

He spoke once more from on the cross . . . a prayer again.

Jesus
Father . . .

Gabriel
See! See! Although abandoned by His Father
     He has maintained the trust.

Jesus
     Father, into Thy hands I commend My spirit.

Gabriel
If you had watched my God at this final moment on the cross,
     you would have seen Him smile,
and I do believe, Jesus knew the smile was for Him.

A signal, now the strain was over and the way was won,
     to start the angel chorus song again.
Softly first, for we would not intrude
     upon the thoughts of God,
     then louder, and more majestic,
          than ever sung before.
     Holy . . . holy . . . holy.
          Lord God Almighty . . .
     who was, and is, and always will be God.
     Thou art worthy, O most mighty Lord,
     to receive from all Thy creatures
          gathered here in heaven,
          and those now redeemed on earth for You,
          and from the Evil One,
     glory and honor and power.
     Thou didst create all things for Thy pleasure.
     Now robed in white in Christ's most holy sacrifice,
     they will bring You pleasure yet again.
     Holy, holy, holy God.

On earth they removed the brutal nails,
     and carried the body to the garden grave.
     They sealed and set the watch,
          lest the disciples snatch the body
          from that hallowed resting place.
And those who loved Him most went home and wept,
     and wept. . . .
God let them weep, but He had news for them
     that would break at Easter's dawn.

To fulfill the Word of Christ, He could not hurry
    with the raising of His Son to life.
It is good to remember those momentous hours,
        even for us angels, for the very heart of God
        grew greater in the doing of them, if that be possible.
And because the great redemption of mankind
        gladdened the heart of God the Father,
        we angels continue to rejoice,
        though we have not ourselves
        profited in any equal measure.
But sometimes I wonder as I look across the great divide
        between where we are who do the Father's bidding,
        and people are, who stand to profit by the Father's love,
        how they can be and do the things they do.

Jesus
Be careful, Gabriel.

Gabriel
Would it help were I to break
        the wall of invisibility between here and there
        and myself denounce them and announce the news
        that there is a way of life,
        made possible by death,
        that leads beyond the end of every person's days?

Jesus
Remember at My death how graves outside Jerusalem
        gave up their dead . . . and none believed . . .
        and how beloved Lazarus returned from death,
        at My command, and how from that day on
            they sought to take My life?
And I, even I came back, returned to life
        by the gentle touch of My Father's hand,
            and they fabricated lies about that miracle.
Do you suppose they would believe an angel,
        however high his rank,
            or myriads of angels?
Besides, this is My Father's plan, that those on earth
        should learn to love Him in return
            for all the love He gives to them.
He maintains the warming sun upon its course,
He sends the rainclouds and the snow
        to break small seeds apart.
But most of all He has decreed

from His judicial stance upon the throne,
that sinners are righteous when their faith
accepts Me as their Savior and their Lord.
The facts are written in the holy Word.
They are in the heart of every faithful friend.
They are abroad in the world on printed page
and all the other media,
and even in the spoken words of some
committed fellow Christians.
This has been Our plan, the recital of the deeds
of Calvary demanded by My Father,
deeds in which I gave Myself as Sacrifice
for the sins of all humanity.
The recital of these deeds should be the call to faith
to sinners under judgment and in danger
of everlasting fire—
that they might be free of condemnation,
to rediscover God the Father,
share in Our lives the blessings
of more abundant living,
and reign with Us in all eternity.

Gabriel

Lord, I hold the trumpet to sound the note
to end the history of earth.
Is it time to sound the call
that will bring Your faithful people
into the light of glory
and destroy their enemies forever?

Jesus

Once I prayed My Father's forgiveness
on the souls of wicked men.
Because I prayed that prayer, the earth remains.
But when the time has come for judgment, it is He who will
give orders for your trumpet blast.

Hold the signal till that time!

Amen.